Revenue Allocation For a Stable Democracy In Nigeria:

Options & Challenges

By Emmanuel Ating Onwioduokit

ISBN 9964 87 548 7

First published 2002 by
African Christian Press
PO Box AH30, Achimota

Editing: Alex Ofori-Karikari
Cover design / typesetting: Kwadwo Osei-Safo

Distributed outside Africa by
African Books Collective
www.africanbookscollective.com

Printed by Lightning Source

Acknowledgement

I am very grateful to a number of people who have contributed to the success of this work. I am particularly grateful to A.H. Ekpo, PhD. Professor of Economics and Vice Chancellor, University of Uyo, who graciously accepted to write the Foreword. Special thanks to Rose Akon, PhD. for useful comments on the first draft of the book.

I want to particularly acknowledge my dutiful secretary, Mr. R.B.Ogundeji for rendering world class secretarial services while the manuscript was being faired. I wish to acknowledge the powerful support of my sweetheart, Mrs. Catherine E. Onwioduokit and my lovely children, Uduak Abasi, Ekemini Abasi, Ubong Abasi and Aniebiet Abasi, for their understanding while the book project took me away from them. My colleague, Mr. Yakubu Aliyu, Research Fellow, Office of the Vice President, Federal Republic of Nigeria, deserves special mention for his encouragement. Finally, I am grateful to God Almighty for sparing my life to see this project to its logical conclusion.

Emmanuel A. Onwioduokit

Dedication

This book is dedicated to the memory of my late father, Chief Gabriel Onwioduokit (Teacher Gabriel) for his total commitment to our education.

Foreword

Revenue Allocation For a Stable Democracy in Nigeria: Options and Challenges has once again re-echoed the importance of properly sorting out of fiscal arrangements between the tiers of government in Nigeria. The author has written the book in a manner in which all stakeholders and others interested in Nigeria's growth and development will understand the subject matter. Though written by an economist, the analysis appeals to a wide spectrum of readers.

The author presents the political and macroeconomic issues in Nigeria in a lucid manner . The chapter on "The Politics of Revenue Allocation in Nigeria" makes the point that revenue allocation is not just an economic matter; it is historical,cultural, social and political. These elements must be considered in any meaningful discussion of revenue allocation in Nigeria.

The chapter dealing with "Options and Challenges for Fiscal Federalism in Nigeria" presents options based on the experiences of Nigeria and elsewhere. Which level of government should collect certain taxes should be seen as both an option and a challenge. The system where all profitable taxes are collected by the centre calls into question the whole debate on fiscal autonomy at lower levels of government.

It is clear that for a stable democracy in Nigeria, the fiscal relationship among the different levels of government must be seriously addressed. This book is quite topical ,especially in the recent debate on resource control. This new book is compulsory reading to all who are interested in Nigeria's emancipation under a democratic dispensation.

Akpan H. Ekpo
Professor of Economics and Vice Chancellor,
University of Uyo

v

Contents

Chapter One

Introduction

The question of how to acquire, increase, allocate and expend revenue constitutes a major issue in the Nigerian Society since its coming into existence in 1914. Before Nigeria's political independence in 1960, the British Colonial Administration handled these issues as it considered fit. During this period, revenue was largely obtained for the establishment and maintenance of infrastructure and to run the colonial bureaucracy. Roads, bridges, railways and sea ports were built to serve the imperialist needs of the colonizing power. The major economic interests in Nigeria represented by such trading outfits as John Holt, and the United African Company (UAC) determined to a large extent who got what, where and when in the economic system. Some scholars have argued that the manner in which revenues were raised and expended under the colonial government may have stimulated the zeal of nationalist pressures for political independence.

After independence in 1960, regionalism became the basis for revenue allocation. The group in power and the regions which they represented became the greatest beneficiaries in the allocation process. Under the parliamentary system of the First Republic (1960-1966) there were three, later four regions. These were the Northern, Eastern, Western and the Mid-Western

Regions. The main economic products of the North were cotton, groundnuts, hides and skin. In the East were palm oil, kernel and timber. The West had cocoa, rubber and timber. These primary products were largely exported to Britain for industrial use. The leaders of the regions and the dominant parties were Nnamdi Azikiwe for the National Council of Nigeria Citizens, (NCNC) in the East, Ahmadu Bello for the Northern People's Congress (NPC) in the North, and Obafemi Awolowo of the Action Group (AG) in the West.

During this period, the dominant principle for revenue allocation was that of derivation. Thus, a sizeable amount of the revenue that was obtained in each region was allocated based principally on the principle of derivation. Although some regions benefited more than others under this criterion, the major actors were satisfied with it. This position changed in the late 1960's when oil became a principal revenue earner. Specifically, oil was found in commercial quantity in the riverine areas of the East and the Mid-West. There were other criteria of revenue sharing in this period. These included the population criterion in which some revenue was allocated according to the population of each of the regions. For this reason, population census became a controversial issue in the country with each region inflating its population for the purpose of attracting more funds. The Federal factor was another criterion for revenue allocation. With this revenue was allocated to the different tiers of government (Federal, State and Local Governments). This criterion suggested that the centre was more important, and so it should have more revenue to meet its constitutional responsibilities such as defence and internal security.

Another criterion was land mass. Revenue was allocated based on the size of land, on the assumption that the larger the size of land, the greater the number of people that occupied it. In the Second Republic (1978-1983), legislators from Borno, Kaduna,

Kano and Sokoto States agitated in favour of a revenue allocation formula that took cognisance of land mass, population and the federal factor. This position was opposed by the then oil producing states of Bendel, Cross River, Rivers and Imo. The problem of searching for an acceptable revenue -sharing formula is always a controversial issue in any country where federalism is the political arrangement. Since 1946 when Sir Richard's Constitution divided the country into three regions, there has been the problem of how to satisfy these regions in the distributive process. As a result of this, various commissions have been set up, from Sir Syndey Phillipson in 1946 down to the Okigbo Commission of 1980. However, none of these commissions, has been able to fashion out an all- time acceptable formula. Consequently, criteria like even development, derivation, equality of states, population, national interest, need, national minimum standard, absorptive capacity, tax effort, fiscal efficiency and total school enrolment have been adopted to suit each area's economic interest.

Altogether, many revenue allocation formulae have been devised since 1946. These include the Sydney Phillips Commission (1946), Hicks-Phillipson Commission (1950), Louis Chick Commission (1954), Raisman Commission (1957), Binn Commission (1965), Dina Commission (1969), Ojetunji Aboyade Commission (1977) and Pius Okigbo Commission (1980). All these commissions were set up in a bid to find a satisfactory means to share revenue but none has been found satisfactory by all the parties concerned. The increasing agitation by the oil- producing areas about the inequalities of the present formula give credence to this fact. There is therefore more urgency to resolve the issue, especially as oil remains the driving force of the Nigerian economy, providing well over 85 per cent of the country's export earnings.

As indicated earlier, the issue of revenue sharing came to sharp focus with the granting of internal autonomy to the regions under the Richard Constitution of 1946 and the subsequent sharing of responsibilities between the national and the regional governments. With this in mind, and to be able to allocate revenue to the regions, the first revenue -allocation Commission was established in 1946 under the chairmanship of Sir Phllipson. The Commission's report was incorporated into the Richards Constitution of that year.

Phillips (1991) opined that in contrast to the allocation of tax jurisdiction, the most frequent changes have been in respect of the allocation of revenue.Thus, Nigeria's revenue allocation system dates back to 1948/49. The revenue sharing formula has been changed for more than ten times during the past three decades - in 1952, 1954, 1956, 1966, 1968, 1969, 1971, 1975, 1980, 1988, 1989, 1992, 1996, 1999 and 2001.

In a debate on the issue of revenue allocation sponsored by the *Daily Times*, Bayode Afode suggested 80 per cent revenue based on population and 20 percent based on the principle of equality of states. The question of derivation was ruled out. But Akiba (1980) identified two major contestants over two major issues in the revenue allocation principle. While the oil- producing states insisted that derivation be made a strong basis for the sharing of the national cake, the non-oil producing states of the country preferred greater weight for the population criterion. These two opposing views were understandable because the South-Eastern States of the country have the mineral resources (oil) but are comparatively deficient in population compared with the non-oil producing states.

The argument of derivation goes beyond moralization as observed by Senator Obi Wali. The principle is much more than mere concessions to communities or states from where revenue sources such as mineral products are derived. To consolidate the stand of the minority oil- producing states, sounds of belligerence tend to be brewing from the extreme flanks . The late Senator Victor Akan argued that "any revenue allocation formula that lacks the lustre of derivation should be taken for a political aberration... a hawkish deal that must be challenged and fought against with vigour". In August 1980, the Governors of Bendel, Rivers and Cross River reached the conclusion that revenue allocation without the principle of derivation was not acceptable.

Alhaji Abubakar Rimi, the then Governor of Kano State was against the derivation principle. He spun around the Bentham school of thought which aims to provide maximum benefits to the greatest number. The population criterion was to him the best and should therefore be given greater weight. He argued that "the success of any government depends on the number of human beings it has catered well for". He accused the derivation campaigners as selfish and unrealistic. For unlike agricultural potentialities which give testimony of the people's hard work on the field, "... oil is natural and never an individual man's making".

Clement Ebri (1980) argued that there is no justification in allocating 20 per cent on-shore revenue to the oil -producing states, and that it is a misnomer to call any single state in Nigeria oil-rich because the resource is natural and inseparable from the geographical placement of Nigeria and its uses ought to be collectively beneficial". Adedeyi (1980) speaking against the principle of derivation, opined that "The derivation principle bedevilled the development of a national and equitable system of revenue allocation in Nigeria. It has poisoned inter-governmental relationships and has exacerbated inter-regional rivalry and conflict. It has hampered the development of the sense of national unity and common citizenship in Nigeria. Moreso, its application has been arbitrary and lacking in consistency. Nigeria must move away from this jacket..."

Okigbo (1980) articulates that Nigeria's mineral Act of 1969 vests in the Federal Government, the total control and ownership of all minerals: "The claim of mineral-producing states to part of the royalties as of right seems to us a fly in the face not only of existing legislation but also of the constitution."

In what appeared to be a highly contested issue, Okon Akiba reacted to Okigbo's position thus: "We have not had the last words on this cake -sharing matter yet, but one remembers that pregnant statement credited to Okigbo early 1980 rather vividly. He said "for any formula on revenue allocation to be acceptable, there should be an interplay of a set of economic judgements and political realizations". Whether he struck a good balance between these two bursting tenets is left for history to determine. One can only observe now that Okigbo's formula has not been that appetizing after all. It has to do with the problem of trying to formulate sound economic policies on slippery political papers.

The Nigerian Federation has been constrained by a number of problems, among which is the issue of an appropriate revenue allocation formula that meets the wishes and aspirations of various interest groups. Within the period of forty years, the Nigerian Federal System has metamorphosed from a two- tier federal arrangement comprising three regions, to a three-tier federal system of 36 states, one federal capital territory, and 774 Local Governments, each of which is constitutionally recognized.

At independence on October 1, 1960, Nigeria had three regional governments - the North, West and East - with Lagos as the Federal Capital. However, by 1963, agitation for self-determination by some minority groups led to the creation of the Mid-West Region with headquarters at Benin city.

As a sequel to the first military coup d'etat of January 15, 1966,

6

which culminated in the civil war, and in order to make for a balanced federation so as to diffuse the fear of domination of certain regions by the others in the country, a twelve-state structure was created out of the then four regions in May 1967. These were, North Western (Sokoto), North-Central (Kaduna), Kano (Kano), North-Eastern (Maiduguri), Benue-Plateau (Jos), West-Central (Illorin), Lagos (Lagos), West (Ibadan), Mid-West (Benin City), East-Central (Enugu), South Eastern (Calabar) and Rivers (Port Harcourt).

Following the military coup that ousted the Gowon regime in 1975 and the need to give identity to the minorities in the Nigeria nation, seven additional states as well as a Federal Capital Territory were created in 1976. The new states were, Bauchi (Bauchi), Benue (Makurdi), Gongola (Yola), Imo (Owerri), Niger (Minna), Ogun (Abeokuta), and Ondo (Akure). In addition, the old states were renamed as: Anambra (Enugu), Bendel (Benin City), Borno (Maiduguri), Cross River (Calabar), Kaduna (Kaduna), Kano (Kano), Kwara (Ilorin), Lagos (Ikeja), Oyo (Ibadan), Plateau (Jos), Rivers (Port Harcourt) and Sokoto (Sokoto). This particular state creation brought the number of states in Nigeria to 19.

Further pressure for new states to meet the yearning of both the minorities and the political interests of the major ethnic groups resulted in the creation of two additional states (Akwa Ibom and Katsina) in 1987, with respective capitals at Uyo and Katsina. This brought the number of states in Nigeria to 21. The states as well as the numbers of local governments within these states are presented below:-

Akwa Ibom(20), Anambra (29), Bauchi (20), Bendel (20), Benue (19), Borno (24), Cross River (8), Kwara (14), Lagos (12), Niger (19), Ogun (12), Ondo (22), Oyo (42), Plateau (16), Rivers (14), and Sokoto (37).

7

In 1991, the political structure was altered significantly when nine additional states were created. These were Abia (Umuahia), Enugu (Enugu), Delta (Asaba), Jigawa (Dutse), Kebbi (Birnin-Kebbi), Kogi (Lokoja), Osun (Oshogbo), Taraba (Jalingo), and Yobe (Damaturu).

By 1996, the military government once again, in an attempt to satisfy the demand for additional states by powerful political and ethnic groups, created six more states. This brought the number of states in Nigeria to 36 . The names of the states, their capitals and the number of local governments are presented below:

S/NO	STATES	CAPITAL	NO OF L/GOVTS
1	Abia	Umuahia	17
2	Adamawa	Yola	21
3	Akwa Ibom	Uyo	31
4	Anambra	Awka	21
5	Bayelsa	Yenegoa	8
6	Bauchi	Bauchi	20
7	Benue	Makurdi	23
8	Borno	Maiduguri	27
9	Cross River	Calabar	18
10	Delta	Asaba	25
11	Ebonyi	Abakaliki	13
12	Edo	Benin City	18

S/NO	STATES	CAPITAL	NO OF L/GOVTS
13	Ekiti	Ado Ekiti	16
14	Enugu	Enugu	17
15	Gombe	Gombe	11
16	Imo	Owerri	27
17	Jigawa	Dutse	27
18	Kaduna	Kaduna	23
19	Kano	Kano	44
20	Katsina	Katsina	34
21	Kebbi	Birnin-Kebbi	21
22	Kogi	Lokoja	21
23	Kwara	Ilorin	16
24	Lagos	Ikeja	20
25	Nassarawa	Lafia	13
26	Niger	Minna	25
27	Ogun	Abeokuta	20
28	Ondo	Akure	18
29	Osun	Osogbo	30
30	Oyo	Ibadan	33
31	Plateau	Jos	17
32	Rivers	Port Harcourt	23
33	Sokoto	Sokoto	23
34	Taraba	Jalingo	16
35	Yobe	Damaturu	17
36	Zamfara	Gasau	14
	*FCT	Abuja	6
Total			774

* *Federal Capital Territory*

However, there are strong indications that the number of States and Local Governments may keep increasing judging from the agitation for more States and local governments by various ethnic groups in the country. The continued agitation for the creation of states and local governments may not be unconnected with the type of fiscal federalism practised in Nigeria. The existing fiscal revenue allocation formula appears to have alienated some segments of the federation, especially the states and local governments, from the control of revenue and expenditure policies, even when the greater part of the revenue is derived from these areas. The operation of what approximates a "unitary system" by successive military regimes in Nigeria has over-concentrated the revenue in the federal government to the detriment of the states and local governments. Thus, it has been argued that the problem in the Niger-Delta ,and indeed the incessant agitation for the creation of more states and local governments, is traceable to the way Nigerian federalism has been managed.

In Nigeria's recent history under military rule, fiscal centralism has stunted the development of the states and local governments and generated increasing bitterness among various communities over perceived inequities in national revenue sharing, especially in oil - producing areas. This is why there has been increasing calls for the use of the principle of derivation for sharing national revenue. The long period of military rule has made government insensitive to the ethics of equitable revenue sharing. The principle of fiscal unitarism fostered on the country by the military has a number of shortcomings.According to Onimode (1999) these include:-

- Local disaffection and perceptions of injustice which may degenerate into local community unrest like the current situation in the Niger-Delta area;

- Weakening of the capacity of the states.

- Stunted economic growth.

- Restive political demands for the restructuring of the federation due to feelings of frustration,

- Social injustice and gradual marginalisation;

- Failure to balance growth and regional development across the country, as the states persistently fail to develop into sustainable growth poles;

- Tendencies towards federal waste and corruption due to the huge resources centralised at the federal level; excessive corruption; official venality and graft are also encouraged by excessive concentration of national resources in a few hands as well as intense, bitter and acrimonious competition for the control of the federal government.

These, among other issues, have rendered the existing revenue allocation formula inadequate as several contending issues that are expected for sustainable federalism are still lacking. This volume seeks to assess these contending issues with a view to highlighting challenges as well as proffering solutions in order to operate a virile and efficient fiscal federalism under a democratic regime.

11

Chapter Two

Political and Macro-Economic Development in Nigeria

A study of revenue allocation in Nigeria is not complete without a preliminary examination of the structure of the Nigerian economy and its political history. The present problem in Nigeria on revenue allocation cannot really be extricated from the structural defects inherent in the economy after independence in 1960, and the subsequent development in political economy.

In Nigeria, political regimes can be segmented into military and civilian. Out of forty years of independence, military regimes have ruled for twenty-eight years. The civilian regime following independence was parliamentary, fashioned after the British model, while the 1979-1983 civilian regime was modelled after the Presidential system of the United States of America. In all the nine different regimes that have presided over the country's political affairs since independence, the military regimes have always seized power after accusing previous regimes (military or civilian) of corruption, nepotism, ineptitude, and the inability to profer solutions to the country's problems. Of the nine political regimes Nigeria has experienced , five have been military, three civilian while one was described as interim. A breakdown of the various political regimes is presented below:

Political Regimes in Nigeria

Period	Type of Government	Head of State
1960 - 1966	Civilian	T. Balewa
1966 - 1975	Military	Y. Gowon
1975 - 1979	Military	M. Muhammed/Obasanjo
1979 - 1983	Civilian	S. Shagari
1983 - 1985	Military	M. Buhari
1985 - 1993	Military	I. Babangida
1993 (Aug-November)	Interim	E. Shonekan
1993 - May 29, 1999	Military	S. Abacha/ A. Abubaka
May 1999 - Date	Civilian	Obasanjo

Each of these regimes had at one time or another acknowledged the need to improve the well-being of Nigerians by stimulating growth and development.

While the first civilian regime (1960-1966) adopted a market-oriented approach to economic management with strong planning and control, the military regime that succeeded it (1966-1975) essentially adopted demand management as the centre-piece of economic policy. The second military regime of M. Muhammed/Obasanjo (1975-1979) opted for a market system moderated by demand management as well as planning and control. The second civilian government (1979-1983) favoured a market system with the introduction of austerity measures to moderate demand. This was continued by the military government of 1983-1985 which also introduced controls and stabilization measures. The Babangida military administration of 1985-1993, heavily tilted towards a market system and introduced the Structural Adjustment Programme which de-emphasized the role of government in economic activities. The brief civilian regime (interim government) led by Shonekan between August and November, 1993 continued with the deregulation policies of the Babangida years. Although the Abacha/Abubakar military administration (1993-May 29, 1999) embraced the market -oriented management philosophy, it introduced another dimension to it; the guided deregulation. However, the Obasanjo democratic regime has in the last two years demonstrated its willingness to liberalize the economy in order to make the private sector the engine of growth.

In all, most of the regimes, whether civilian or military, in Nigeria have played major roles in the Nigerian economy. The outcome of their economic policies have been extensively discussed elsewhere by Onwioduokit (1998).

From independence, Nigeria was basically an agrarian society, with agriculture accounting for at least 65 per cent of GDP. The contribution of the sector however declined markedly until it reached an all-time low of 17 per cent in 1982. Crude Petroleum came on the economic scene significantly in 1970 when Nigeria became a member of the Organization of Petroleum Exporting Countries (OPEC). From then on, oil became the mainstay of the Nigerian economy.

The oil boom of the early 1970s had a pervasive effect on the growth and development of the economy. Oil suddenly became the dominant sector of the economy, accounting for more than 90 per cent of exports, and the main source of revenue. Between 1972 and 1974, federal revenue from oil increased fivefold, contributing about 80 per cent of total revenue.

14

Nigeria's new wealth substantially affected the scope and content of investment, production, and consumption patterns, the government's approach to economic management, and the policies and programmes implemented. Federal expenditure doubled between 1973 and 1974, and between 1974 and 1975, much of the increase in expenditure went to investment. At 1984 prices, the share of investment in GDP rose from 12 per cent in 1971 to more than 25 per cent in 1977.

The growth in oil revenue was largely absorbed by public sector spending particularly on transportation and social services. Transportation facilities, especially roads and ports, were expanded radically, as were educational opportunities. However, many public projects were undertaken without the requisite analysis of their long-term financial viability and the efficiency with which such projects were implemented in the past. This development altered the underlying structure of the economy. High wage and price increases secured goods, but they depressed the non-oil traded goods sector. Nigeria borrowed significantly during this period to purchase foreign goods. Economic problems began to manifest in 1978, but a second oil boom in 1979 lent credence to the assumption that oil revenue would in fact be a sound basis for planning and sustaining public sector consumption and investment.

The second oil boom coincided with the civilian government of the second Republic , yet the economic problems persisted. In 1980/81, the terms of trade doubled from their 1976 level. The increased oil revenue gave impetus to the government to increase public expenditure, leading eventually to a deficit in 1980.

Overall, GDP recorded a growth of 4.2 per cent in 1980. In 1981, oil prices fell precipitously. Thus, adverse terms of trade variation led to extraordinary fluctuations in real income. Because the oil boom could not generate enough revenue to keep

15

pace with public expenditure, real income declined and the government was forced to run a budget deficit and increase its borrowing. By 1983, the Federal budget deficit amounted to 12 per cent of GDP.

The government financed its external and fiscal imbalances by incurring debt, depleting international reserves, and going into arrears in external commitment. Unfortunately for the country, real World interest rates turned positive when its term of trade started to deteriorate. An exchange rate policy that allowed the Naira to appreciate with rising oil revenue in tandem with rising domestic costs meant a sharp deterioration in international competitiveness, thus impacting negatively on the agricultural sector.

Despite the increased expenditures occasioned by the increased oil revenue, the federal government still maintained a budgetary surplus. However, in 1976, expenditure began to outstrip revenue. Also, state budgets began to record deficits as federal government transfers to states declined from 40 per cent of federal revenues in 1973 to about 20 per cent in 1979. Furthermore, in the non-traded goods sector, wages were inflated to keep pace with that offered in the construction and service sectors. Meanwhile, the value of the real exchange rate increased by more than 93 per cent from 1973 to 1978. The continued appreciation of the Naira placed exports at a disadvantaged position.

Foreign exchange from oil was used to increase the supply of tradables. Nevertheless, import demands were greater than what oil earnings could accommodate, hence, since additional debt could only be contracted at variable interest rates and at shorter maturities, credit conditions became less favourable. In the early 1980s, real interest rate reached 20 per cent. Given the poor rates of return on investment in Nigeria proxied by a negative GDP growth rate during the period, the country undertook massive external borrowing.

Despite the precipitous drop in oil revenue the real exchange rate continued to appreciate. The distorted exchange rate prevented the government from allocating resources efficiently to purchase imports, hence the government established several measures and stringent trade controls in the Economic Stabilization Act of 1982. Among the measures were the rationing of foreign exchange, and a restriction on the import deposit programme. Also, public investment was cut drastically, and petroleum product prices and tariffs were raised.

In spite of these austere measures, the economy reached a crisis point in 1983/84, when oil prices declined markedly by 45 percent from the 1980 level. In 1983 the GDP recorded a negative growth rate of 6.7 per cent; the external current account deficit was 6 per cent of GDP and the budget deficit/GDP ratio reached 13 per cent.

In all, external and fiscal imbalances emerged, Nigeria's indebtedness impeded her access to foreign capital and short -term trade arrears accumulated to the point at which foreign banks held back on confirming letters of credit. However, given the country's unwillingness to devalue the Naira, creditors refused to roll over short- term debts, or to provide fresh capital. It was under this precarious condition that the military again seized power in December, 1983.

The military government augmented the austere measures of 1982, imposed a wage freeze on public sector employees, enforced the redundancy of a large number of civil servants and introduced user fees in the education and health sectors. These measures made a minimal impact on the budget deficit, which dropped from 13 per cent of GDP in 1983 to about 3 per cent in 1984. However, the regime while cutting funds for maintaining infrastructure and equipment, continued to fund inefficient parastatals.

17

The decline in public expenditure affected adversely the construction and service sectors. Production and employment declined sharply in most other sectors of the economy. Capacity utilization declined and plant closures were widespread as access of the import-dependent industrial sector to imported inputs was sharply curtailed. Imports and non-oil exports declined by 22.7 and 44.2 per cent, respectively in 1984.

The declines in imports and exports were accompanied by a significant rise in domestic price levels, and the inflation rate rose to 40 percent. Domestic savings and investment fell; investment fell to 12 per cent of GDP, down from 24 per cent in 1981.Private investment also fell significantly by 25 per cent in 1985. External debt service requirements reached 34 per cent of exports of goods and non -factor services in 1985.

By 1985, the distortions in the economy were severe and varied. The exchange rate was still grossly overvalued, the budget deficits experienced in the earlier year were still prevalent and import controls were made more stringent. In addition, the government could not reach an agreement with the Bretton Woods Institutions on several issues including devaluation of the Naira and import liberalization. Significant differences thus emerged between the Nigerian government and its creditors.

It was while this deadlock ensued that the Babangida government seized power in August 1985. The government proclaimed a fifteen-month period of national economic emergency from October 1985. By 1986, the terms of trade had plummeted to about 35 per cent of their 1980 level. Moreover without proper accommodation to multilateral lending institutions, the prospects for further credit were bleak. These events necessitated the adoption of a Structural Adjustment Programme in 1986.

The Structural Adjustment Programme (SAP) adopted by the Babangida administration introduced far -reaching reforms in the

18

Nigerian economy: the exchange rate was devalued; interest rates were liberalized; imports and exports were also liberalized. In addition several public enterprises were either commercialized or privatized. These developments led to a reverse trend in the Nigerian economy; the declining trend in the GDP growth rate between 1986 and 1993 were consistently positive, though at varying levels. (See Faruquee, 1994).

Following the annulment of the June 12, 1993 presidential election, the military Head of State, Ibrahim Babangida, stepped aside from power and installed an interim government to conclude the protracted transitional programmes being pursued by his regime. However, in November 1993, there was another military coup that sacked the interim government, dismantled all democratic structures, and reversed as it were, the economic reform policies being pursued by the interim government. In 1994, there was a major shift from liberalization to control in economic management. This development resulted in major macroeconomic misrunnings.

Inflation rates worsened reaching a crisis level of 72 per cent in 1995. The interest rate reforms failed to yield the desired results because of frequent policy changes. Given the high inflation rate, the real interest rate consistently maintained a negative level even with the adoption of SAP.

In Nigeria, starting from 1995, the foreign exchange market, interest rate, and direct foreign investment were liberalized; these were accomplished through the Autonomous Foreign Exchange Market (AFEM), the abrogation of the Enterprise Promotion Decree of 1979, the Exchange Control Act of 1962 and the liberalization of the interest rate. The banking system was prudently restructured to ensure soundness and transparency. The 1997 monetary and banking policies which adumbrated in the Federal Budget, the restruction of the entire financial system, and the

19

fiscal surplus achieved in 1996, appear to have seemingly approximated the precondition for efficient economic development. However, the need to sustain and improve the enabling environment through the unification of the exchange rate, further consolidation of growth, reduction in external indebtedness through a restructuring programme agreeable to the Bretton Woods Institution that could illicit a favourable disposition by our creditors in ensuring debt reduction for Nigeria, was paramount. In 1998 the government phased out the multiple exchange rate arrangement and adopted a market -oriented exchange rate regime. With the coming into office of the Obasanjo democratic government, the issue of corruption and other forms of malpractices are being tackled through the introduction of the Anti-corruption Act of 1999. It is expected that with this development, the confidence of foreign investors in the Nigerian economy would be greatly enhanced. Thus, the Nigerian economy could be said to be on the right track to eventual recovery.

Chapter Three

Theoretical and Conceptual Issues

Federalism is a process of unifying power within a cluster of states and decentralizing power within the unified states. The essence of this is the coexistence of unity with the determination not to smother local identity and local power. Federations usually possess constitutions which ideally provide for a polycentric political system where there are numbers of centres of decision-making, each centre being formally independent of the other(s) and bearing responsibility for some basic social services and development schemes, (Ramphal, 1976).This ideal case which emphasizes decentralisation, notwithstanding, some scholars have noted that the dynamics of the relevant society, to a very large extent, determines the form the federation takes; whether the tendency is towards greater centralization or decentralisation of power (see Onazi, 1999). In summary, fiscal federalism exists when sub-national governments have the power, given by the constitution or by particular laws, to raise (some) taxes and carry out spending activities within clearly -established legal criteria (Tanzi, 1995). The main economic justification for decentralization centres principally on allocative or efficiency grounds.

There is also the political argument for decentralization if a country's population is not homogeneous and if ethnic, racial, cultural, linguistic or other relevant characteristics are regionally distributed. Decentralization is usually employed to induce various regions to remain part of a federation. In a democratic setting the economic and political argument for centralization blend into each other, and so it could be argued that decentralization strengthens democracy. It is believed that people are more inclined to engage in local political activities because local policies have a more direct impact on their day to day life.

Cremer, Estache, and Seabright (1995) observed that the Normative economic arguments for decentralization are based on both an ex-ante and the expost cases. While Oates (1972) is seen as the leader of the ex-ante, Tiebout's (1956) work essentially form the basic focus for the expost case.

Oates' case is based on the fact that not all public goods have similar spatial characteristics. Some, such as defense, benefit the entire country. Others, such as regional transportation systems or forestry services, benefit regions. Furthermore, others such as street lighting or dimming, benefit only municipalities or particular districts. Moreover, different areas have different preferences for public goods. Thus the supply of public goods must be fitted to the different groups. A centralized government might ignore these capital characteristics and this diversity of preference, or it might not be well informed about them and thus might supply a uniform package to all citizens. A one-size- fits-all approach does not deliver a basket of public goods that is optimal for all citizens. But, when the jurisdiction that determines the level of provision of each public good includes precisely the set of individuals who consume the good , there is perfect correspondence in provision of public goods. This Normative Model in theory would require a highly -decentralized public sector with many subnational jurisdictions of varying sizes.

Thus, each level of government possessing complete knowledge of the taste of its constituents, and seeking to maximize their welfare, would provide the pareto-efficient level of output which would be financed through benefit and efficient pricing. Thus for the public good , the consumption of which is defined over geographical subsets of the total population, and for which the costs of providing each level of output of the good in each jurisdiction are the same for the central or the respective local government , it will always be more efficient for the central or the respective local governments to provide the pareto-efficient levels of output for their respective jurisdictions than for the central government to provide any specified and uniform level of output across all the jurisdictions.

In sum, decentralization has been advanced on the grounds that centralization is costly if it leads the government to provide a bundle of public good different from the preferences of the citizens of a particular region, province or municipality. If these preferences vary geographically, a uniform package chosen by a national government would possibly lead some localities to consume more or less than they would prefer to consume. Consequently, for the sake of efficiency,each type of public good should be provided by a level of government enjoying a comparative advantage in accounting for the diversity of preferences in its choice of service delivery (Cremer, et al 1994).

Decentralization has been defended on the basis of other, more practical considerations. It has been argued that a decentralized system can become a surrogate for competition, bringing to the public, some of the allocative benefits that a competitive market brings to the private sector. There are many angles to this argument. Tiebort (1956) however maintains that the final outcome will approach that of an efficient market to the extent that decentralization can help identify different population groups' preference for the public goods. Local governments supply these goods; these groups can be made to pay a price based on the benefit they receive from the public goods, and individuals vote with their feet, by moving to the jurisdiction that best reflects their preferences. At the margin, the benefit from consuming the public goods or service will be equal to the cost in terms of benefits taxes, thus approaching a pareto-optimal solution (Tanzi, 1995).

Decentralization allows for experimentation in the provision of the output. When the provision of public service is the responsibility of local jurisdictions and when these jurisdictions are free to provide the service in any appropriate way, some jurisdictions will discover better ways of providing the service and other jurisdictions will emulate the successful ones. The more jurisdictions there are, the more simultaneous experiments will take place. When the service is imposed by a national monopoly, which adopts a uniform approach to providing the service, there will be little or no experimentation, and thus outdated methods may continue to be used even when there are better alternatives.

Decentralization is expected to confer on individuals who are responsible for the result of their actions, and who thus have ownership rights over the outcome, stronger incentives to perform better. Thus, when local officials are directly responsible for providing a public service, and are praised for success and blamed for failure, they will have a greater interest in succeeding. In such cases, the community may develop a sense of pride in successful service delivery. Furthermore, when the cost of providing a service is borne by the local jurisdiction, the service is more likely to be provided cost-efficiently. Shaw and Qureshi (1994) in supporting this view opined that accountability brings responsibility and motivates much of the support for the decentralization of various functions. Indeed, Brennam and Buchaman (1980) noted that at the time when large public sectors are considered wasteful and inefficient, decentralization is desirable because it is likely to be associated with a smaller public sector and a more efficient economy.

However, the above potential benefits of decentralization may be reduced or even disappear if the minimum public expenditure management infrastructure is not in place. In addition to the revenue they raise from their own tax bases, fees, resources, and shared revenue, sub-national governments often depend on grants from the central government. They often can make a strong case for these grants because the national government may require them to perform certain functions or to comply with certain standards without directly providing funds for them. Such unfunded mandates create implicit claims for future grants for soft budgets. Designing an optimal grant structure is very difficult. Thus, as observed by Bahl and Linm (1992), grants may introduce inefficiencies and create political pressures to increase their size.

Fiscal decentralization may however aggravate structural fiscal problems through several channels. The literature identifies three main channels namely : the assignment of major tax bases, the expost and implicit servicing of debt incurred by subnational governments (Tanzi 1995).

In some decentralized countries major tax bases are assigned to sub-national governments for their exclusive use. For instance, in Brazil the general value-added tax is assigned to the states while in India, it is the sales tax that is assigned to the states. However, in Russia, personal income tax and many excise taxes have been assigned to the sub-national government. If the tax bases that are assigned exclusively to sub-national governments are large and dynamic, and if the spending responsibilities of central governments cannot be easily compressed, macroeconomic problems are often inevitable. When macroeconomic adjustment

25

requires that a central government increases its tax levels, it will find it difficult to do so if important tax bases are not available to it. In this situation, the central government may be forced to rely on less optimal tax bases. Consequently either the level of taxation would be lower than desired or the structure of taxation would be less efficient than it could be.

While some tax bases are assigned to the exclusive use of particular levels of government, other tax bases may be shared. The sharing is usually of two kinds. Different levels of government may tax the same base or one level may collect the tax from a given base and share the revenue with other levels.

When two government levels tax the same tax base, each retains its independence of action even though an increase by one level in its dependence on that base may limit the scope for the other level to tax the same base. At the sub-national level the limits on effective tax rates on a given tax base are generally imposed by tax competition and by the potential mobility of the tax base.

These sharing arrangements, which are limited to specific taxes rather than to the entire tax revenue, also have important efficiency implications on the revenue side. The central government that finds itself in great need of raising revenue but also has to share some tax revenue with sub-national governments would have a strong incentive to raise revenue from the taxes that are not shared or from taxes that would go mostly to the central government. As a result the structure of the tax system would be distorted, and unshared taxes would acquire a greater weight in the tax system even when they are less efficient. However, when tax sharing applies to total tax revenue, rather than to specific taxes, these problems tend to become less serious.

With regard to borrowing by sub-national governments, if strictly applied, constitutional limitations prevent sub-national governments from borrowing if the market is able to impose discipline on borrowing by sub-national governments. If national governments never intervene when a sub-national government gets into trouble then borrowing by sub-national jurisdictions does not contribute to a country's macroeconomic difficulties. However, very few countries have such strict constitutional limitations, markets have proven unable to discipline borrowing, and central governments are often unable to refuse assistance to sub-national governments that get into trouble.

There are several reasons for this unhappy outcome in a sub-national government's financial problems. In some cases it has to do with revenue assignments that do not match expenditure assignments.

Conceptually, fiscal operations of any economy can be perceived from two extreme forms of public sector. On one hand, there exists a highly-decentralized fiscal system in which the government at the centre has no economic responsibilities ; the other levels of government on the other hand perform virtually all economic functions. The other extreme is a case of total centralization where the central government undertakes complete responsibility for all economic activities of the public sectors and thus, no other tier of government participates in the economic life of the nation. In reality, there exists some degree of decentralization in all economies (Ekpo and Nbebbio, 1996). In discussing the issue of decentralization, Ubogu, (1982), noted that an operational measure of decentralization is the share of decentralized expenditures and revenues of the state and local governments in the nation's total fiscal activities. Musgrave (1972) opined that within the context of expenditure centralization, allowances should be made for the degree of central direction of local expenditures. Specifically, he emphasized that expenditure made at the local level may not be only centrally financed but also centrally directed. Local governments which act as central expenditure agents do not reflect expenditure decentralized between the federal and state governments, but relatively centralized at the local governments level (Ekpo, et al, 1996). Consequently, the extent of centralization directly affects the tax structure. Some taxes are administered more efficiently at the central level, while others are better managed at the state and local governments levels. Thus, the extent of tax centralization impacts on the development effort of an economy.

There appears to be a consensus in literature that centralization of government expenditure is directly related to rising per capita national income. Peackock and Wiseman, (1961) hinge this proposition on the fact that as economic development occurs, there would be increasing urbanization which will put pressure on government to provide greater service. The major principles of fiscal federalism could be stylised as follows:-

- Expenditure assignment must precede the assignment of tax power,

- Each public service should be provided by the jurisdiction having control of the minimum geographic area that would internalise the benefits and costs of such provision.

- This arrangement calls for maximum decentralization of services delivered on the grounds of efficiency, accountability, manageability and local autonomy. Nevertheless, where a good generates substantial spatial externalities in terms of benefits and costs to non-residents, or where the economies of scale are larger than a local jurisdiction or where there are substantial compliance and administrative costs, a more centralised provision could be preferred;

- Policy functions dealing with stabilization (e.g. monetary policy) and redistribution policies can only be carried out

28

at the national level and

- It is possible to make a distinction between the technical production of a good and the mere political function of provision of a good or service, via contracting arrangements.

The implications of the above in terms of the allocation of responsibilities between the tiers of governments in a federal system are enormous. On the revenue side, each level of government should be assigned tax sources commensurate with its responsibilities. Nevertheless, it is essential to reconcile considerations of efficiency (minimization of resource cut) with equity (nationalization of expenditure and revenue heads). In that regard, seven basic principles are advocated.

- Progressive redistributive taxes should be central;

- Taxes suitable for economic stabilization should be central, lower level taxes should be cyclically stable;

- Tax bases distributed highly unequal between jurisdictions should be centralised;

- Taxes on mobile factors of production are best administered at the centre;

- Residence based such as sales of consumption goods to consumers or excise are suitable for states;

- Taxes on completely immobile factors are best for the local level; and

- Benefit, taxes and user charges must be appropriately used at all levels (Mussgrave, 1972).

However, as noted by Onimode (1999), the long period of military rule in Nigeria had given rise to fiscal unitarism with the concomitant problem of high military extraction. Thus for most of the period of military misrule in Nigeria, fiscal federalism deviated markedly from the theoretical expectations outlined above.

However, with the return to a democratic system of government, it is expected that the practice of fiscal federalism in Nigeria should to a reasonable extent approximate the theoretical expectations so as to make for the balanced development of Nigeria.

Chapter Four

The Politics of Revenue Allocation in Nigeria

The question of how revenue should be shared among the tiers of government in Nigeria is as old as Nigeria itself. It is one which every government in Nigeria has had to grapple with but which has remained seemingly intractable. David Ejoor, in **Reminiscences** states that the minorities have not had their fair share of the national wealth and that the avenue for an equitable distribution must be found.

Hans J. Morgenthau in **Politics Among Nations**, identifies balance of power as only a manifestation of a general social principle to which all societies, composed of a number of autonomous units, owe the autonomy of their component parts, that the balance of power and policy aiming at its preservation are not only inevitable but are essential stabilizing factors in a society of sovereign nations ... The concept of equilibrium as a synonym for *"balance"* is commonly used in many sciences - Physics, Biology, Economics, Political Science and Sociology. Here, our interest is not on how it affects these sciences but rather on how it affects the economy and political situation in Nigeria.

The problem of imbalance has been with us since the colonial times . This reflected mostly in the economic sector where the North and the West dominated the economy of the country with the East trailing behind with only palm produce as their main export product. The advent of oil as the main source of revenue in the country at the time that agriculture lost its grip accentuated the widening imbalance.

In 1953 when the Northern People's Congress (NPC) and the Action Group (AG) presented a common front for a more decentralised federal structure, the National Council of Nigerian Citizens (NCNC), in opposition, argued against this, demanding instead a rather more centralised framework of government. The two contending positions were reflected in the proposals submitted to the commission on revenue allocation which was set up in that year to examine the fiscal implication of the constitutional changes then. The Action Group wanted revenue allocation between the component units of the federation on the basis of derivation. Cocoa was the main revenue earner for the country. They threatened that the West would break away if their demand was not met. Granting that demand gave the Action Group and the West an edge over the other three regional governments.

Unlike the Action Group (AG), the Northern People'sCongress (NPC) representing the North, wanted revenue allocation on a per capita basis which would have favoured the North with its 'larger' population. The National Council of Nigerian Citizens (NCNC) representing the East on the other hand, being fiscally worse off, wanted revenue allocation on the basis of need, taking a position with regards to the functional division of power between the federal government and the regional governments. This position the National Council of Nigeria Citizens had maintained in 1957 when another Commission on Revenue Allocation was instituted in consonance with further changes envisaged in the constitution then.

In 1964, however, when the prospects of oil had made the East the most favourably placed regional government in the federation, the National Council of Nigeria Citizens (NCNC), no longer needed the federal structure it had long championed. Hence, when another Commission on revenue allocation was set up in 1964, the National Council of Nigeria Citizens, in its memorandum, argued in favour of a "loose" federal structure, a position somewhat similar to that of the Northern People's Congress in 1953.

Furthermore, this inadequacy in allocation made the NCNC in 1964 to see itself as worse off in the scheme of things. The NCNC statement in that year corroborates this assertion:

Take a look at what they (i.e. the Northern People's Congress) have done with the little power we surrendered to them to preserve a unity which does not exist. Kanji Dam project - about N150 million of our money when completed, all in the North. Bornu Railway extension, about N75 million of our money when completed, all in the North; spending our N50 million on the Northern (SIC) Nigerian Army in the name of a Federal Republic; Military Training and all ammunition factories and installations are based in the North, thereby using our money to train Northerners to fight Southerners, building of a road to link the dam site and Sokoto Cement Works N7million when completed, all in the North; total on all these four projects is about N262 million. Now they have refused to allow the building of an iron and steel industry in the East and paid experts to produce a distorted report.

33

One of the allegations against the federal government by the dissident groups in the April 22 1990 abortive coup was the question of power imbalance with a particular area dominating the affairs of the government thereby hijacking the country's resources to that area. They saw this as cheating the revenue-producing areas which incidentally are mostly inhabited by minorities relegated to the background. For instance, the situation in Akwa Ibom State where the politics of off-shore oil dichotomy is at play, represents a precarious example. This has increased the imbalance in terms of employment and compensation of the oil - producing states. The whole matter reinforces the claim that there has been an element of politics in revenue sharing in Nigeria.

The problem associated with evolving an acceptable revenue allocation formula for the country has not just surfaced today. One recalls that the issue of revenue allocation in Nigeria came into sharp focus with the granting of internal autonomy to the regions under the Richards Constitution of 1946 and the consequent sharing of responsibilities between the national and regional governments. The issue is even more complicated now with the creation of more states thereby making revenue allocation in the country a thing of great concern.

As part of the fourth year anniversary of the Babangida administration on August 27, 1989 the President announced to the nation that after careful consideration of the report of the Danjuma Commision, the Federal Government decided to establish the National Revenue Mobilisation, Allocation and Fiscal Commission, which was vested with the power,

a)   To monitor the accruals to and disbursement of revenue from the federation account;

b)   To review from time to time the revenue allocation formulae and principles in operation to ensure conformity with changing realities;

c)   To advise the federal, state and local governments on fiscal efficiency and methods by which their revenue can be increased.

d)   To determine the remuneration appropriate for political office holders, including the President, Vice-President, Governors, Deputy Governors, Ministers, Commissioers, Special Advisers, Legislators, Chairman, Vice Chairman and Councillors of Local Government Councils;

e)   To make recommendations as provided for under Section 82, 122 and 160(8) of the 1989 Constitution and;

f)   To discharge such other functions as may be conferred on it by the Constitution or any other Act of the National Assembly.

The fact that the Commission was given a permanent status goes further to buttress the dynamic nature of revenue allocation in a federation.

Political and Economic Dimensions of Revenue Allocation in Nigeria

The Political Dimension

Since revenue allocation became very political, especially with the discovery of oil as a major source of revenue for government, there is now a basket of criteria used in determining how to allocate the nation's revenue. Land mass is one of such criteria. The people of the oil- producing states which form the minority have always opposed the stereotype, orthodoxy and contemporary political and social life of the Western and Northern Nigeria with its monolithic leviathan, its stifling bureaucracy, its gag on minorities which in effect, has made them (minorities) to remain perpetual hewers of wood and drawers of water for their political overlords.

This push for further self-determination, the spirit of micro-nationalism within a federating entity has caused a lot of anxiety for government. But it has also readily brought into focus the problems of unbalanced federalism in general and the danger inherent in any central authority administering in such a way as to give its components cause to believe that there is second -class treatment in a federation that is built on the classical understanding of equal opportunities and equal development.

Another area in which the minorities seem to have made gains is in the aspect of state creation. The strength of the minorities multiplied when Murtala Muhammed increased the number of states to nineteen (19). Babangida further strengthened the hands of the minorities with the 30 state structure because nearly half of this number are dominated by the minorities. What the creation of more states has done has been to bring more equity into the distribution of national wealth and power. Development of the minority areas could now be better attended to. But the continual neglect of the need for self-determination in Nigeria, especially by the minorities, has resulted in several uprisings and wanton destruction of life and property. The case of the Ogoni nine is a classical point in view.

The Economic Dimension
Nigeria, with an economic base which is almost solely sponsored by crude oil, is also battling with the hazards of tottering international markets. At home there are questions to answer over the consolidation of natural wealth and the distribution of the scarce resources therein. The economic issue has really never produced any unanimity among the minorities. In fact, it tends to show how complex the situation is. According to Tam David-West, former Petroleum Minister, there is "not much live (fight)

or die common grounds between the Northern minorities and the Southern minorities", especially on the issue. He added that on the issue of revenue disbursement:

> *"Southern oil-producing minorities want the principle of derivation, while the Northern minorities prefer land mass...There must be non-negotiable common grounds regardless of smaller local-interest considerations".*

Negotiating the common ground is the problem. The Southern minorities are of the view that their oil money is used in developing the North, including the Northern minority areas and the majority groups. The Northern minorities on the other hand, are not sure that the oil-producing states in the South can really lay claim to owning crude oil discovered off-shore. Besides, there is always the argument that nearly all the heavy industries associated with the oil industry are sited in the Southern minority states.

Essentially, in an economy made up of smaller and heterogeneous fiscal units, the constitution defines the powers each level of government has to raise taxes and similar charges. However, one authority may have the power to raise or impose certain taxes and charges while the power to collect them is reposed in another authority. In addition, the rights to the revenue collected may be given in full or in part to an authority different from the one that imposes the tax and charges. Therefore, the right to the revenues raised by the different levels of government involves the redistribution of fiscal resources among the various tiers of government.

The distribution of the central government's resources among the different levels of government is an issue of major policy concern in virtually every developing nation. The allocation of Federal revenues is rationalised in a number of ways: to compensate states and/or local governments for limited taxing powers; to brace local governments to bear the substantial public cost of rapid urbanisation; to reduce inter-governmental income inequality and to carry out national government planning with respect to the stimulation of economic activity in various states and/or governments within the country.

In other words, the argument posited for transferring revenues from higher to lower tiers of government in a federation include:-

a)   Balancing or deficiency transfers, that is, transfers necessitated by an imbalance between revenues and responsibilities;

b)   Equalisation transfers, that is, transfer necessitated by variations in the revenue-raising capacities of the lower levels of government such that heavier tax burdens in the lower levels of government are eliminated; and

c)   Situation incentive or promotional transfer, that is, transfers which are regarded as functional or conditional in that they are made with specific directives as to their disbursement.

There is no gainsaying the fact that a complex casual connection exists between Nigeria's revenue allocation (and in fact, fiscal arrangements as a whole) and constitutional arrangements. In this sense, one agrees with Teriba (1966) that

> *"developments and innovations in fiscal arrangement have, in general, been dictated by the tenure and pace of constitutional changes and transformation by the latter is also, in turn occasionally influenced by the former".*

From this perspective, it is clear that revenue allocation is a dynamic process which changes with the historical and political conditions of the country. It is in this regard that revenue allocation becomes unsuitable for detailed constitutional pre-scription, hence only general guidelines can be stipulated in the constitution. Such guidelines include taxing power, what consti-tute public revenues, authority to disburse and/or approve the dis-bursement of public revenues, etc.

Subsequently, the allocation of resources has changed over time and all the changes focus at equitable distribution of the resources to all groups that make up the nation. This is to consolidate the achievements made so far in opening up the rural areas and to provide potable water and basic health facilities to the rural areas.

It is clear that whatever formula that is evolved will be contro-versial since it is not possible to satisfy everybody at the same time. Babangida, after seizing political power in 1985 and acknowledging the problem in 1988, when he inaugurated the 9 member National Revenue Mobilisation Allocation and Fiscal Commission, noted that the issue would always be contentious until a stable political system is developed. The Commission, which was headed by retired Lieutenant-General Theophilus Danjuma, was given the mandate to devise an effective process for mobilisation of resources of public revenue, periodic review of revenue allocation principles and formula to reduce political pressures on allocation of national resources, among others.

In order to determine the justice or otherwise of the revenue allocation issue, it is pertinent for us to also examine the various factors that influenced the inclusion of a federal character prin-ciple in both the 1979 and 1989 Constitutions, respectively. Federal Character refers to the reflection of all component units within the federation in all governmental activities. According to Ukwu I. Ukwu (1985),

"it is a principle designed to promote national unity, foster national loyalty and give every citizen of

"Nigeria a sense of belonging to the nation, notwithstanding the diversities of ethnic origin, culture, language or religion which exist among them."

As provided in Section 14 Sub-section 3 of the 1979 Constitution.

"The composition of the government of the federation or any of its agencies and the conduct of its affairs shall be carried out in such a manner as to reflect the federal character of Nigeria and the need to promote national unity, and also command national loyalty thereby ensuring that there shall be no predominance of persons from a few states or from a few ethnic or sectional groups in that government or in any of its agencies".

According to J. Isawa (1980) "The essence of this provision was to create a sense of belonging to the state's involvement in the government and a mechanism for extracting commitment and loyalty for citizens regardless of their ethnic base". To him, exclusion of any section of the community from participation and sharing in the national resources could alienate them and create a sense of apathy.

The Babangida administration laid great emphasis on the usage of the federal character concept and this was by way of correcting the practices of the past, especially in the conduct of public management which tended to exploit negatively the diversities of the nation thereby causing ill will. It was equally a reaction to those practices that tended to project selfish and parochial considerations, which placed self interest (i.e. tribal and state) over and above the interest of the nation. Thus, the concept of federal character has always been seen as a deliberate design to construct and devise a means of ensuring the proper and equitable allocation of resources in the country. Throughout the life-span of that administration, the formula was changed five times. In 1992 alone, it was changed twice. Needless to add that all these alterations were aimed at the decentralisation of the government. Prior to that time, the allocation of these resources did not so much take into account the interest of the revenue- yielding states. For instance, until June 1992 when the allocation to the oil producing states was increased from 1.5 per cent to 3 per cent ,most of the oil-producing areas in the country showed signs of underdevelopment compared to other areas. That is to say that resources were taken from some states and channelled to other states for development purposes.

In May, 1992 when Babangida attended the 25th anniversary of the creation of Rivers State, he promised that something would be done positively to ameliorate the pains and hardship faced by the oil-producing states. In the following month changes were made. That was indeed commendable of that administration.

41

Chapter Five

Revenue Sharing Between the Centre and the States in Nigeria

Prior to 1946, the issue of revenue sharing raised no serious national concern since there was real fusion of fiscal operations in the country. With the coming into effect of the Richard's Constitution of 1946, which provided for a Legislative Council for the whole country and Regional Councils with large measures of devolution, the issue of revenue sharing came into sharp focus. Consequently, various revenue allocation commissions were set up at different times to examine the issue of revenue sharing between the centre (Federal Government) and the regions (the states) and among the regions and local governments. Among these commissions were the Philipson Commission (1946) the Hicks-Philipson Commissions (1951), Sir Louis Chick Commission (1953), Sir Jeremy Raisman Commission (1958), the Binn Commission (1964), the Dina Commission (1968), the Aboyade Commission (1978) and the Okigbo Commission (1980). The first ever Revenue Allocation Commission which was appointed in 1946 was headed by Sir Sydney Phllipson. The Commission was

---

1 E.C Amcheazi (ed), Reading in Social Sciences: Issues in National Development (Enugu: Fourth Dimension, 1980, pp. 38-53)

2 For detailed discussions on this recommendations of these commissions see II. Ukpong, Notes on Nigeria's Fiscal Policy (Uyo: Oduduma, 1984) pp. 10-12

to relate revenue allocation to political changes as dictated by the Richard's Constitution. It proposed a fiscal arrangement which sought to concentrate fiscal powers in the national government. While the bulk of the Nigerian revenue was collected and retained by the national government, the region had to rely on "block grants" from the central government. Such block grants were made only after the recurrent and capital expenditures of the central government had been met. It was the central government that determined the size of the grant using the formula:

$A = R - (g+r+s) - E$
Where A = central grants to the region
R = Total Nigerian revenue
g = grants received under the colonial developments and welfare Act
r = aggregate declared revenue of the region
s = estimated budget surplus of the central government
E = total expenditure of the central governments.

   In addition, the regions were granted some independent sources of revenue which consisted of the region's share of the revenue from direct taxes collected by the Native Authorities from licences, mining rents, fees of courts, rent from government property and earnings from government departments. These constituted the "declared" revenue of the regions. No doubt, this fiscal arrangement left the region in a miserable financial position which precipitated the clamour for more fiscal and constitutional reforms. Consequently, the Hick Philippson Fiscal Commission was set up in 1951 following the granting of a quasi federal structure for Nigeria. To broaden the revenue base of the regions, additional regional taxes were introduced. These included sales tax on motor spirits, tax on tobacco and entertainment tax. To qualify as a regional tax, the tax must be clearly localised within the region, must have stable revenue yields, must be inexpensive to administer and must not endanger national interest and policy. On the whole, the fiscal arrangement under the Hicks Phillipson Commission made for significant improvement in the revenue position of the regions. When Nigeria became a full-fledged federation in 1954, there was the need to marry the fiscal powers of the different levels of government, with their statutory responsibilities under the new constitution. Thus, the Louis Chicks Commission was set up in 1953 to work out a fiscal arrangement that would ensure "that the total revenue available to Nigeria are allocated in such a way that the principle of derivation was followed to the fullest degree compatible with meeting of the reasonable needs of the central and each of the regions". The Commission made a strong case for an increased financial might of the federal government. Accordingly only the revenue collected by the federal government in excess of its own needs was allocated to the regions in accordance with the principle of derivation. This arrangement was informed by the following:

i)   If the federal government was to be independent of the regional government within its own sphere and also coordinate them, it must have its own revenues;

ii)   As economic development of Nigeria would depend in a large measure upon the financial resources of the federal government, its reasonable needs must be viewed generally and its present reserves must not be distributed lavishly to the regions.

However, between 1954 and 1966, a number of measures were introduced which whittled down the financial strength of the federal government and increased the revenue position of the regions. Among these measures were the following:

i)   The tenacious adherence to the principle of derivation.

ii)   Under Raisman recommendation, the regions were allowed full share of the proceeds from export taxes, import and excise duties with the federal government receiving the share attributable to consumption in Lagos;

iii)   Regionalization of Marketing Boards: This means that the surpluses accumulated by these boards were retained by the respective regional governments. Besides, the regions were free to fix producer prices and to impose sales tax on the produce of the marketing boards. This, apart from accentuating regional revenue disparity, also reduced drastically the revenue accruing to the federal government from export taxes;

iv)   The introduction of Income Tax in the Region: The Jeremy Raisman Revenue Commission set up in 1957 recommended complete regional jurisdiction over the personal income tax. This was supposed to give the regions control of an expanding sources of revenue.

v)   The increase in revenue from mining rents and royalties (which at that time was under regional jurisdiction); as a result of increase in petroleum production and exports.

The implication of this lopsided revenue allocation system was that while the regions were very strong and buoyant the federal government was becoming too weak to perform its crucial role of stabilising the political system. The fiscal relationship between the federal and regional or state governments changed dramatically with the emergence of military governments in Nigeria. The Federal Military government, on assumption of power in 1966 introduced measures which gradually eroded the financial powers of the regions so that by 1979, the states were left with less than 25 per cent of the total revenue. Under the military arrangement, the following measures were put in place:

a) The federal government collected and retained in full, company income tax, petroleum profit tax and excise duties. State governments share from royalties were reduced from 100 per cent to 50 per cent.

b) Revenues from excise duties on sale of tobacco and petroleum products and import on motor spirits previously paid to the states on the basis of relative consumption were shared equally between the federal government and the Distribution Pool Account (DPA);

c) Export duties previously allocated wholly to the state by derivation were shared in the ratio of 3:2 by the state of origin and the DPA;

d) The introduction of the offshore oil Revenue Decree No 9 of 1971 under which offshore oil revenue went entirely to the federal government further whittled down the revenue base of the regions;

e) The abolition of Marketing Boards which were the principal source of revenue to the states and their replacement by Commodity Boards;

f) Introduction of a uniform tax structure on personal income tax and sales tax in 1975 meant that the states could no longer vary these tax rates in response to their needs; and

g) The retention by the federal government of revenue accruing from petroleum profit tax and excise duties, even though both accounted for more than 60 per cent of the federally collected tax revenue in the 1975 fiscal year.

As part of the transition to the Second Republic, the Federal Military Government appointed the Aboyade Technical Commission on Revenue Allocation in 1977, to review the inter-governmental tax jurisdiction and revenue allocation arrangement with a view to injecting better efficiency in the working of fiscal federalism. Based on the principles of fiscal efficiency and economy, the Aboyade Report recommended the delineation of functions as follows:-

1)   Federal Government:
a)   Defence and Security
b)   External Affairs
c)   Inter-State and International Roads
d)   Railways
e)   Airport and Facilities
f)   Power Supplies
g)   Communications
h)   Heavy Industries
i)   Higher Education

II)   State Government
a)   Secondary Education
b)   Urban Water Supply
c)   Housing
d)   Health
e)   Lighter Infrastructure and Industries
f)   Agriculture
g)   Town and Country Planning

III)   Local Government
a)   Sewage Disposal
b)   Maintenance and Feeder Roads
c)   Primary Education
d)   Market Stalls
e)   Rural Health
f)   Craft and Small Scale Industries

The report then considered which levels of government should have jurisdiction over which taxes, and resolved the tax jurisdiction of the three tiers of government as follows:

I)   Federal Government:
a)   Import Duties
b)   Export Duties
c)   Excise Duties
d)   Mining Rents and Royalties
e)   Petroleum Profit Tax
f)   Companies gains Tax (Legal Basis Only)
g)   Personal Income Tax (Legal Basis Only)
h)   Personal Income Tax of Armed Forces Personnel,
i)   External Affairs Officers and Federal Capital Territory
j)   Sales and Purchases Tax (Legal Basis)
k)   Stamp duties (Legal Basis Only)

II   State Government
a)   Sales or Purchase Taxes (Except on Commodities so designed by the federal government administration and retention).
b)   Football pools and other Betting Taxes
c)   Estate duties
d)   Gift Tax
e)   Land Tax (Other than Agriculture Land)
f)   Land Tax (Legal Basis Only)
g)   Land Registration (Legal Basis Only)
h)   Capital Gains Tax (Administration & Retention)
i)   Personal Income Tax (Administration & Retention)
j)   Company Tax (Administration Only)
k)   Stamp Duties (Administration & Retention)

III   Local Government
a)   Property Tax
b)   Market and Trading Licences and Fees
c)   Motor Park Dues
d)   Entertainment Tax
e)   Motor Vehicle Tax and Driver's Licence Fees
f)   Land Registration (Administration & Retention).
g)   Licence fees on T.V. and Radio (Administration and Retention)

The Committee examined the basis of revenue allocation in the country, and recommended that all the revenues collected by the federal government, without exception, be paid into the Federation Account to be shared among the Federal, States and Local Governments in the ratio of 60 per cent, 30 per cent and 10 per cent, respectively.

It has been observed that the Aboyade Report recommendations were based on considerations for economy and efficiency in tax administration. The Committee was, therefore, more concerned with setting up more effective administration and fiscal controls than had hitherto existed. The report, therefore, concluded with recommending a special panel to study the ways and means of improving the machinery for tax assessment and collection.

The Aboyade Committee was faced with a situation in which the Federal Government enjoyed a relative and apparently comfortable financial position which made it to increasingly take over the traditional functions of the States and Local Governments. Examples were in Agriculture, Health, Water Supplies, Primary Education, Health Care and other rural development projects. This situation made the Aboyade Committee to recommend that all Federally-collected revenue (except the personal income tax of the Armed Forces, External Affairs Officers and FCT) should be consolidated into one account to be shared by the Federal,

States and Local Governments in the following proportions:

Federal Government	-	57 per cent
State Government	-	30 per cent
Local Governments	-	10 per cent
Special Grants Account	-	3 per cent

The proportions above represent the respective shares of each level of government in the allocation of revenue from the Federation Account. It was the belief of the Committee, after a careful examination of the Constitutional functions assigned to each tier of government, the independent revenue sources available to each, and the total federally-collected revenue minus the specified portion retained by the Federal Government (as its independent revenue), that such a system would guarantee an adequate revenue base to each tier of government.

In addition to the 10 per cent of the Local Government, each state was also to contribute 10 per cent of its total internal revenue receipts to the share of its constituent Local Governments from its fund. The special grants account was meant to cater for problems requiring special provision, such as oil pollution, general national ecological problems, national emergencies and disasters. The Report also recommended five (5) principles for the sharing of revenue from the State Joint Account.

The principles are:-

i)   Equality and access to development opportunities;
ii)   National Minimum Standards for National Integration;
iii)   Absorptive Capacity;
iv)   Independent revenue and minimum tax effort; and
v)   Fiscal efficiency.

These principles represent a combination of equity and efficiency measures, allowing for the minimisation of the development gaps among states, the (Absorptive) capacity of states to make full use of funds (an expenditure index), the ability of each tier of government to realize its potential taxable capacity in respect of those revenue sources within its jurisdictions and the minimisation of the costs of operating government functions. Finally, the Committee recommended that the establishment of a Joint Fiscal and Planning tax jurisdiction as well as the principles governing the relative shares of the   respective tiers of government which were to last until 1980, be put in place. Other traditional sources of revenue for each tier of government remained as they were prior to the Aboyade Report.

Although the Federal Military Government modified and accepted the Aboyade Report but differed in its implementation due to the enormous computational work involved, the Constituent Assembly rejected the recommendation of the Aboyade Committee on the grounds of the practicability of applying most of the principles for revenue sharing among the state and local governments. However, most of the recommendations of the Aboyade Committee were later implemented by the Federal Military Government.

Barely a month after assuming office, President Shagari, on November 21, 1979 appointed an eight-man Presidential Commission to harmonize   the deliberation at the Constituent Assembly on the need to ensure that each tier of government had adequate revenue to discharge its constitutional function. The terms of reference were basically to ensure a   high degree of correspondence between governmental responsibilities on the one hand, and revenue sources, on the other. The Committee was also to examine the revenue allocation formula and make appropriate recommendations. The Committee examined the levels of expenditure by each tier of government (both recurrent and capital), which were then used as a basis for determining the relative weights, in financial terms, of responsibilities of the different tiers of government. These weights were then applied in the vertical revenue allocation scheme.

The weights were modified following the recognition that some functions (listed in the 1979 Constitution) that were previously the exclusive reponsiblities of states and local governments (e.g. Primary Education, Health, Agriculture, etc.) had been taken over by the Federal Government. It followed therefore that any changes in the constitutional responsibilities of any tier of government would have a significant effect on the relative shares of allocable revenues.

On the basis of these observations, the Okigbo Committee recommended that the Federation Account should be shared in the following proportions:

Federal Government	-	53 per cent
State Government	-	30 per cent
Local Government	-	10 per cent
Special funds to be Applied as follows:-		
Initial Development FCT	-	2.5 per cent
Mineral Producing Areas	-	2.0 per cent
Ecological & Other Disasters	-	1.0 per cent
Revenue Equalization Fund	-	1.5 per cent

Thus, although the State and Local Governments' share of the Federation Account was 40 per cent, the same as their combined weight of expenditure on constitutional functions, the distribution between them had changed. The States' shares declined from 37 per cent to 30 per cent while the Local Government's share remained at 10 per cent. Similarly, the Federal Government's net expenditure weight of 60 per cent was reduced to 53 per cent and the difference assigned to the Special Fund Account.

The Okigbo Committee acknowledged that a satisfactory allocation system should strive to satisfy the twin objectives of equity and efficiency, strengthen the effort of the Federal

Government to manage the national economy, ensure adequate financial flows to the State and Local Governments as well as being capable of quickly adjusting to changing circumstances. Following the Government's White Paper on Okigbo's report, the 1981 Allocation of Revenue (Federation Account) Act was enacted by the National Assembly. This Act was amended in 1984 by a Decree, raising the share of the states from 30.5 per cent to 32.5 per cent.

While the Aboyade Report had recommended that all Federal revenue should be subject to the Allocation Scheme it also advised that the (30 per cent) share of the States should be shared among them according to the following criteria:

Criteria	Relative Importance
Equality of Access to Development Opportunities	25%
National Minimum Standards for National Integration	22%
Absorptive Capacity	20%
Independent Revenue	18%
Tax effort Fiscal Efficiency	15%

The Okigbo Report however recommended different factors and weights as follows:

	%	Gwp	1981 Act	1984 Amendment
(i) Minimum Responsibility of Government	10.0	10.0%	40.0%	40.0%
(ii) Population	40.0	40.0%	40.0%	40.0%
(iii) Social Development: Factor (a) Primary School Enrolment of which: direct enrolment inverse enrolment	11.25 3.75		11.25% 3.75%	11.25% 3.75%
(v) Internal Revenue effort	5%		5%	5%
	100.0		100.0	100.0

The report also recommended that the sharing of revenue among the Local Governments within the states should be on the same principles and the weights by which revenue is shared among the states. By this, each State Government was expected to contribute 50 per cent of the State Governments' total (Internal Revenue) to the State Joint Local Governments Account (SJLGA) for sharing among the Local Governments in the State. Moreover, to integrate the Local Government into the vertical revenue sharing arrangement, efforts were made in the committee's recommendations to ensure that the constitutional responsibilities of each tier of government were supported by independent revenue resources as well as adequate share of the total revenue.

From the above, it was obvious that the federal government assumed almost complete control of revenue matters in the country. Thus, while the Federal Government had so much money that it could implement the gigantic Universal Primary Education Scheme and host the FESTAC '77, the state governments were so financially paralysed that they could hardly pay monthly wage bills of their workers. The states were therefore, heavily dependent on the federal government for "block grants" to supplement their meagre revenue position. This state of affairs did not just offend the principle of fiscal federalism but also produced a near unitary system of government in Nigeria.

Since 1981, revenue sharing between the Federal Government and the States has followed the provision of the 1981 Revenue Allocation Act. The Act was a follow-up to the recommendations of the Okigbo Revenue Allocation Committee set up in 1980 to work out a more acceptable formula for revenue sharing in the light of the changing functions of the various levels of government under the new Presidential Constitution. The fiscal arrangement under the Act allowed for a revenue-sharing formula which gave the Federal Government 55 per cent of the total revenue, the state governments 35 per cent, and the local governments 10 per cent. Of the 35 per cent share of the state, 30.5 per cent went directly to the states based on an approved formula, 2.0 per cent was to be shared to the states on the basis of derivation, 1.5 per cent for the development of mineral producing states and 1.0 per cent for the amelioration of ecological pro- blems. For the first time, local governments were given a direct allocation from the Federation Account. In 1987, the Federal Military Government altered the revenue allocation formula to the effect that while the Federal and local Governments maintained percentage shares of 55.0 and 10.0 per cent, respectively, the state governments' percentage share fell by 2.0 per cent. The special fund's share rose from 0.5 per cent to 2.5 per cent.The development of mineral producing areas was allocated 1.5 per cent, just as the general ecology share was

1.0 per cent. This arrangement was further tinkered with unilaterally by the Military in 1990 thus, the Federal Government's share was reduced from 55 per cent to 50 per cent, while the state governments' share was reduced by 2.5 per cent to 30 per cent. However, the local government, Special Funds, as well as all other sub headings maintained the 1987 level. In 1992, the Federal Government adopted yet another revenue sharing formula. By that arrangement, the Federal Government' share reduced to 48.5 percent, while state governments' share fell by 6 per cent to 24.0 percent. On the one hand, the local government's share rose by 100 per cent to 20 per cent while Special Funds allocation increased to 7.5 per cent. The percentage allocation to Federal Capital Territory, Derivation and Stabilisation remained at 1.0, 1.0 and 0.5 percent, respectively. However, the allocation to Development of Mineral producing Areas and General Ecology were 3.0 and 2.0 percent, respectively.

On the 19th of August 2001, the Revenue Mobilisation, Allocation and Fiscal Commission, submitted a new formula to the federal government. In the new arrangement, the federation account was proposed to be allocated among the various tiers of government in Nigeria using the following formula:

Vertical Allocation

Federal Government	41.3 per cent
State Government	31.0 per cent
Local Government	16.0 per cent
Basic Education/Skills Acquisition	7.0 per cent
National Reserve Fund	1.0 per cent
Agriculture/Solid Mineral and Science Development Fund	1.5 per cent
Federal Capital Territory Development	1.2 per cent
Ecological Fund	1.0 per cent

Horizontal Allocation

Equality of States and Local Governments	45.0 per cent
Population	25.0 per cent
Internal Revenue Efforts	8.0 per cent
Education	1.5 per cent
Health	4.0 per cent
Terrain	5.0 per cent
Rural roads/inland water ways	1.5 per cent
Derivation	13.0 per cent

(To be shared among the states and local governments benefitting from the fund):

States	60 per cent
Local Government	40 per cent

The proposed revenue allocation formula is not desirable. It appears that the proponents of the new formula have not learnt anything from our political history. A few examples will suffice; the assignment of the weight of 25 per cent to population is bound to take us back to a situation where for purposes of revenue allocation benefits, most states inflated their population figures. There is no reason to believe that, that situation will not continue, thereby making our ability as a nation to have an accurate and reliable population census a mirage. Indeed, population is an asset and not a liability, consequently it will be more desirable to target less controversial weights that would in the short to long run impact positively on the quality of life of the populace.

Again, fixing the derivation at 13 per cent is not acceptable. The Constitution says "not less than 13.0 per cent". The argument that the Commission followed constitutional provisions fly in the face of fact. While we agree that education is desirable and in fact an imperative, one could not justify the inclusion of education in the weight, when there is education tax fund that should take care of education. However, if education must be included, it should be to finance the educational needs of those who are already enrolled in school. This will act as an incentive for states to ensure that their enrolment figures increase over time. Internal revenue efforts seems to be out of place. In its place, it would be desirable to have the states collect the value added tax and share it between the states and local governments within the states on the basis of 60 : 40 per cent. The Federal government should not be included in the VAT sharing as it has other viable sources of independent revenue.

In sum, we recommend that population for political reasons should be assigned 5.0 per cent weight, while the remaining 20 per centage point is shared among other weights as follows;

(1)   Derivation 10 additional per centage point to make the assigned weight 23 per cent

(2)   Rural roads/Inland waterway - additional 5 per centage point to make the weight assigned 6.5 per cent.

(3)   Terrain and Health should be assigned additional 2.5 per centage points each to raise the respective weights to 7.5 and 6.5 per cent.

Clearly, the existing formula (as well as the proposed formula) has reduced the Federal government's share of the total revenue from the federation accounts compared to the 1970s, but what is not clear is whether the reduction is significant enough to make the state less dependent on the centre. It appears the existing formula still favours the Federal Government more than the State governments. While a financially strong Federal Government is necessary in order to maintain political stability and national unity, there is a legitimate fear that excessive flooding of the central government with funds could lead to wasteful spending and exacerbate uneven development. Indeed, most analysts have linked the alarming rate of corruption in Nigeria to the excessive funding at the Federal government level. The same argument goes for the *life and death* struggle for political power at the centre in Nigeria.

Chapter Six

Revenue Allocation Formula and Constitutional Responsibilities of Tiers of Government

In Nigeria, the existing formulae, like the previous formulae, especially in relation to the vertical factors and their weight, are contentious for one singular reason. They have been manifestly proven as either totally lacking in any conscious attempt at, or are less than altruistic in matching the shared responsibilities of the three tiers of government with the need to providing a commensurate revenue base to meet the expenditure obligations inherent in them. Each allocation formula seems to have successively been designed to serve the central government alone, whether in inter-governmental negotiations or in the management of the economic and fiscal resources of the Nigerian nation state. Our history is replete with awful incidences of the violation of the constitutionally-assigned powers of the peripheral structures by the central government through the manipulation of the vertical factors and their weights in the allocation of revenue.

It is in the interest of an enduring democratic culture that the vertical factors and their weights in revenue allocation be predicated on the essential logic of matching the shared responsibilities of the tiers of government with the need to affording them with commensurate revenue base to meet the expenditure obligations.

In this regard, let us focus on contemporary issues of fiscal federalism in Nigeria basing our analysis on the 1999 Federal Constitution. The constitutionally assigned responsibilities of each tier of government under this Constitution is summarized thus:

A)   **Federal Government:**
i)   Defence and Security
ii)   Foreign Affairs
iii)   Inter State and Inter-National Roads
iv)   Port facilities
v)   Railways
vi)   Airport and facilities
vii)   Power Supply
viii)   Communications
ix)   Higher Education

B)   **State Governments:**
i)   Higher Education
ii)   Secondary Education
iii)   Primary Education (i.e. maintenance of standards, co-ordination, certification, etc).
iv)   Market Stalls
v)   Rural Health (i.e. Primary Health Care)
vi)   Crafts and Small-scale Industries

C) Local Governments:
i)   Feeder Roads
ii) Maintenance of primary schools
iii) Maintenance of primary health centres

Analysis of Responsibility Profile
A) Federal Government:

As indicated earlier, the profile of constitutionally assigned responsibilities reveal that, the Federal Government appropriated all the essentially economic and financially viable functions of state. The other peripheral structures of State and Local Governments are saddled with basically social national agenda. Other than defence and security; and foreign affairs, to some extent, every other item in the profile of responsibility of the Federal Government generates revenue through which, each is or ought to be self-sustaining and self-supporting. In effect, the Federal government is not required in strict logic of economics to spend extra funds. In what follows, we shall attempt to analyse each of these variables, for instance:

i)   Inter-State and International Routes have toll gates and revenue is thus generated for their maintenance. If well managed, considerable surplus funds outside the residual maintenance charge on toll gate revenue, should accrue to the Federal Government from this source.

ii)   Port Facilities, both seaports and airports attract fees

iii)   Railways, the rigidities of its management in Nigeria not withstanding, is a unique form of transportation which if well managed, should generate enough revenue to at least cover maintenance and other charges. It ought to be self sustaining.

iv)   Power supply, though still managed by a government monopoly, with effective delivery of services should be self sustaining. Nevertheless, despite its poor showing today, the volume of investment in physical infrastructure bear eloquent testimony to its financial muscles.

v)   Communications, whether internal or external, are fee-charging services for all classes of users.

vi)   Heavy-industries, the point has to be made that heavy industries are strategic to the industrialization drive of any country. However, the return on investment on them, when functional, justifies the huge financial outlay of their establishment. Heavy industries are potentially profitable.

vii)   Higher Education is a responsibility of the Federal Government. It is a statutory compulsion for the Federal Government to establish any number of strata of Higher hospitals, for example, they tend to attract rich patients and thus collect higher fees. The essential advantage almost exclusively enjoyed by the teaching hospitals is that they attract the elite class capable of paying reasonable fees for the treatment of any kind of ailment. In a related case, the Federal Government has not established enough higher educational institutions. Consequently, the states are compelled to respond to the inadequacy of space for their indigenes and have taken upon themselves the responsibility of establishing colleges of education - polytechnics, universities, etc.

B)   State Government
The constitution seems to have saddled the states with the responsibility of providing essential social services which require huge capital outlays but without reason-

able prospects of generating revenue . A few examples will suffice:

i)   Higher Education, as indicated earlier, is not sufficiently provided by the Federal Government. Thus, the States are compelled to provide higher education for their indigenes. This choice involves a huge capital commitment to an area that is essentially Federal Government responsibility. This leaves the States with less resources as they have no areas of profitable returns to offset investment in this sector.

ii)   Secondary Education is capital intensive and is assigned basically to the State Government. Huge financial commitments are made annually in the construction and maintenance of secondary schools. In an effort to encourage this level of education, some state governments have abolished schools fees, thus facilitating greater access to this level of education. However, even where fees are collected, empirical findings show that not enough is realised to maintain the infrastructure and meet the running costs.

iii)   Urban/Rural water supply whose returns on investment in Nigeria is almost negligible, is rather capital intensive. In rural areas in particular, given the level of poverty and the essential nature of water supply, most states cannot but subsidise water supply to the rural areas. In effect ,not much revenue is usually realised that could cover the preliminary cost o f rendering this service.

iv)   Housing is one area in which income could have been generated. However, due to the skewed revenue allocation formula, the State Governments do not have enough funds to embark on Housing projects which could have been sold at a future date to the people. Thus, both the people and state suffer on both counts.

v)   Healthcare delivery is an essential social service. Bed charges and other fees payable by the ordinary citizens who need medical services from State Government hospitals are, without dispute, inadequate to make up for the financial outlay initially expended on hospitals. On the other hand, denying the citizenry access to health care because they cannot pay for it immediately is not comformable to civilized practice since the citizens are potential creators of wealth. Given this dilemma, most health sectors managed by State governments do not have a veritable revenue base.

vi)   Intra-State and intra-city roads are not yet sources of funds, since tolls are not collected on them. On the contrary, some states spend significant amount of their funds in providing intra-city roads annually. At face value, this is basically a welfarist programme and does not yield any returns at all.

vii)   Agriculture has a dual purpose: to provide food for the teeming population and to feed the industries with raw materials. However, our agriculture is still struggling to fully meet the objective of providing food for our population. The absence of a solid and well-developed industrial base vitiates the second objective. Thus, the prospect of agriculture generating revenue is, to all intents and purposes, futuristic.

viii)   Town and Country planning is very revealing of the incongruity in the shared responsibilities among the Federal, State and Local Governments. It is the State governents that plan the urban centres and countryside.

65

But tenement rates derivable from erected physical structures, if residential, are paid to the local governments, and if industrial rates are paid to the Federal Government, the State governments get nothing. In addition, given the poor state of the environment, State governments are compelled to provide drainage and sewage facilities for the disposal of solid waste, sewage and industrial effluents. This is capital intensive, yet the States have no statutory revenue sub-head to pursue such programmes.

C)   Local Governments:

Other than the feeder roads, the Local Governments derive revenue from every other aspect of their assigned responsibilities. Indeed, the Local Governments are basically at the gaining end of the investments of the State governments in education and health. Now, the Local Governments do not seem to bother themselves with any other responsibility than the payment of teachers salaries. They do not seem to concern themselves with maintenance of the infrastructures of the primary schools, primary health centres, etc. However, without prejudice to our earlier analysis, we believe that more responsibilities should be devoted to the Local Government, but this should be preceded by adequate staffing with competent personnel.

There are no generally acceptable and all - time applicable formula for revenue sharing among states of the federation. As mentioned earlier, the various Revenue Commissions set up at one time or the other had recommended different formulae for revenue sharing in the country.

We shall now examine some of the commonly used criteria for inter-state revenue sharing in Nigeria.

1. **The Principle of Derivation**

    This was the first criterion to be used for revenue allocation in Nigeria. It was first introduced by the Philipson Commission in 1964. The principle states that each state's share from the central revenue should be proportional to its contributions to the centrally collected revenue. This principle has been in use in all the revenue allocation formulae for the country, although with varying degree of emphasis. For instance, in the Phillipson and Chicks recommendations, the principle of derivation had overriding consideration. In Dina, Aboyade and Okigbo Commissions, the principle attracted a very significant weight. Generally, there has been a progressive decline in the emphasis given to derivation in the Nigerian reveenue allocation formulae. In the 1950s, it attracted almost 100 per cent, but declined to 20 per cent in 1975 and 2 per cent from 1991 to 1998, but increased to about 13 per cent in 2001.

    Advantages

1. One outstanding benefit of this principle is that it promotes fiscal efficiency. Since the states know that their share of the revenue depends on their ability to generate the revenue, they will strive to maximize the yields from the available tax sources.

2. It promotes the production of export crops. In the 1950s and 1960s, when the principle was applied, it encouraged the regional governments to promote the cultivation of export crops such as cocoa, palm kernel, cotton, ctc. from this point of view, the use of the derivation promoted efficiency through the direct contribution of the states to the generation of revenue.

3.   The principle is also advocated on equity grounds. It is argued that it is equitable for states from which the bulk of the revenue is obtained to obtain an extra share beyond what any other states receive.

4.   The derivation principles is also acclaimed for promoting efficiency in resource allocation. States that produce the products that are in high demand should be encou - raged to produce more by allocating more revenue to such states. The principle of derivation allows states to rigouorously exploit the various resources within their jurisdiction. At the same time, the principle produces the necessary sanction on states that would want "to reap where they did not sow".

5.   One of the arguments given by Sir Phillipson for advocating the principle of derivation was that it will "train the regions in the art of cutting their coats according to their cloth and inculcate in them a sense of financial responsibility".

Disadvantages

1.   The principle aggravates regional disparity in revenue and income. When derivation was introduced in the 1950s, it benefited the West more than other regions because they controlled the bulk of the export crops and also had the highest record of tobacco consumption. States that could not produce export crops were put in a perpetual state of penury.

2.   While the principle of derivation works well in a loose federation, it has been found to be unsuitable for a closely -knit federation. It tends to emphasize state differences, make the poor states suspicious of the rich and create a general feeling of disharmony and acrimony.

3. For the principle of derivation to work properly, there should be good and reliable statistical data. The contribution of each state to total revenue and output and the tax yields from the different tax sources must be clearly known. The arbitrary assignment of weights is bound to produce an unfair pattern of income distribution.

4. The principle introduces elements of instability into the revenue position of the states. In years where the yield from agricultural exports were low, the tax revenue to the state: producing such crops fell.

II.   The Principle of Need

The principle of need, like that of derivation, is a very popular criterion for interstate revenue allocation. It has been consistently used by successive commissions with varying emphasis. For instance, the Dina Commission assigned 50 per cent while Okigbo accorded it 40 per cent. This criterion emphasizes the fact that each state should be able to cater for the basic needs of its citizens. On the basis of this principle, each state receives federally- collected revenue according to its individual needs. One good indication of need is the population. The main advantage of this principle is that it is easy to compute, since in a normal situation the population of each state can be easily ascertained from the national census figure. Secondly, it promotes equity and makes for a more even distribution of income. Thirdly, it reduces social disharmony in the society since all and sundry are catered for on the basis of their number.

However, the use of need as a basis for revenue sharing is inhibited by a number of problems:

i)   It is a qualitative index and prone to subjective interpre-
      tation;

ii)   The Population figure in Nigeria is highly unreliable
      to be used as an index for revenue sharing; and

iii) It may impair economic development since the productive
      states are not given enough encouragement.

III   Balanced Development
One of the conditions for a healthy development of a
federal state is that the disparity in income levels among
the states should be minimal. In other words, no single
state should be so strong financially or so developed
economically as to constitute a threat to other states.
A good revenue formula must seek to reduce any fiscal
imbalance within the federation. Even development has
been repeatedly mentioned by the various fiscal commissions in the country. The criterion promotes national
unity, removes regional disparity in income and promotes healthy competition in the states. However, major
set backs of the criterion include:

i)   No acceptable index of the relative level of develop-
      ment;

ii)   Absence of data on per capita income per state; and

iii) The measures of even development used which include;

a)   The social development factor (Okigbo, 15 per cent)

b)   The national minimum standard (Aboyade, 22 per cent)

Currently, what is used as a proxy for the social development
factor is enrolment in the primary schools. However, it is recog-
nised that social development is multi-faceted and so primary
education alone is a poor proxy for it. But in deciding what other

70

factors of social development should be included, one has to consider the ready availability of data. On the strength of this, other indicators of social development such as health and water were posited in recent times. The best indicator of social development is the health delivery services. But there are no readily available data for these. The second best measure is the number of hospital beds available per 100 persons in each state. Also, as regards health services, there is the need to consider both the maintenance of the existing hospital facilities as well as the encouragement to set up additional ones. As such, the health component of the index of the social development factor should have both direct and inverse relationships. In the same vein, the availability of good water should be incorporated into the social development factor.

IV.   Internal Revenue Effort

This is referred to as fiscal efficiency criterion or independent tax effort. Using this criterion, the greater the internal revenue, the greater the share of the revenue. In most literature on revenue allocation in Nigeria, it is asserted that the best measure of the Internal Revenue Effort is to relate internally generated revenue to the potential taxable capacity. But it is also pointed out that in the absence of GDP or disposable income figures on a state by state basis, the potential taxable capacity of each state cannot be measured. Thus, the Internal Revenue Effort cannot be measured in the most ideal way.

Yet, there is every reason to encourage the state governments to do everything possible to increase their internally generated revenue. And in view of the fact that it may take some time before the statistics for measuring Internal Revenue Efforts are

71

available, other proxies to measure the efforts of the state governments in tapping their internal sources of revenue are posited. In particular, this author is proposing an incremental approach to the measurement of the internal revenue effort. The percentage increase in internally generated revenue in a given period over the preceding period, should be taken as a measure of the internal revenue effort for the period. Admittedly, it could be argued that for states that are close to maximum efficiency in revenue collection, additional efforts would result in only a marginal increase in revenue, while for states that are presently very inefficient in revenue collection, very little effort would result in a phenomenal increase in revenue. Also, if two states are compared, one with a large revenue collection and the other with a small revenue collection in absolute terms, a large increase in revenue in absolute terms may still represent a smaller percentage increase in revenue in the case of the former than a smaller increase in revenue in absolute terms in the case of the latter. In these respects, the measure of the internal revenue effort would appear to penalize states that have already attained reasonable efficiency in revenue collection as well as states that are already collecting large amounts of revenue in absolute terms. However, in the final analysis what is important is overall increase in aggregate revenue collection. If it therefore takes a little bit of "favouritism" to cajole states that are not so efficient in revenue collection to increase their revenue collection efforts, the inequity could be excused.

Chapter Seven

Revenue-Expenditure Profile of Government

As noted earlier, there has been a limited degree of fiscal decentralization in Nigeria. With the 1954 constitution that was essentially federal in nature, regional and state governments were given traditional responsibilities with separate and independent budgets. However, the revenues from regional or state taxes remained grossly inadequate to meet their expenditure responsibilities. Consequently, states usually depended on their share of federally collected revenues, while the federal government retained fiscal supremacy. Between 1954 and 1974, the bulk of revenue made available to the regional and state governments was on the basis of derivation. This was believed to have mirrored the essentials of federalism. However, in 1975, when government believed that the then existing revenue allocation formula exacerbated regional disparities in the level of development, the tendency toward the equalization principle emerged. Nevertheless, over time more resources were made available to the states and local governments, but the large portion of the federally collected revenue continued to be retained by the central government. Revenue available to the three tiers of government in Nigeria comprises tax and non-tax financial flows which are derived from internal and external sources. The internal sources are those revenue sub-heads constitutionally assigned to the three tiers of government, whereas the external source is made up of statutory revenue allocation from the federation accounts, discretionary grants, and value added tax.

As indicated earlier, while the major revenue heads in the country, such as customs duties, mining rents and royalties, petroleum profit tax and company income tax all of which account for about 82 per cent of total national recurrent revenues, between 1980 and 1988, fell under the legislative and administrative purview of the federal government the less productive and less buoyant sources were ceded to the fiscal jurisdiction of state and local governments.

A cursory perusal of the sources of revenue to governments in Nigeria as indicated in table 2 reveal that between 1990 and 1998, the share of the federal government in total revenue averaged 65.7 per cent of the total revenue. The states' share on the average stood at 28.6 per cent. The share of local government during the period averaged 5.7 per cent.

It is clear that the bulk of revenue during the reviewed period went to the federal government. Thus, the issue of revenue decentralization in Nigeria has not been effective. It should however be noted that the application of this conclusion should be taken with caution since the data point is limited to the decade of the 1990s. This was on purpose, since the local government's direct allocation from the federation account only started in 1993. Thus, the analysis here is basically for the purpose of illustration.

Aggregate federally collected revenue rose astronomically from N634.0 million in 1970 to N8,042.4 million in 1977, but declined by N671.4 million from the 1977 levels to N7,371.0 million in 1978. By 1979, the revenue figure increased by 48.0 per cent to

N10,912.4 million. The trend continued up till 1981. Between 1972 and 1978, the revenue fluctuated between N11,433.7 and N27,596.7 million. It maintained an upward movement to N520,190.00 in 1996. As shown in table 2, the federation account dominated the current revenue of the state governments from 1985 to 1998. The structure of local government revenue from 1993 to 1998, (the period when consolidated data were available) shows that external sources of funds, mainly allocation from the federation account, constituted over 91 per cent of their current revenue. This is a clear reflection of fiscal imba-lance in the distribution of functions and revenue sources.

There has been a significant shift in the structure of federally collected revenue over the years. For instance, while non-oil revenue contributed N254.4 million to total revenue in 1970, oil contributed N166.6 million. By the end of the decades of the 1970's, the structure changed significantly. Thus, by 1979, total non-oil revenue contributed N203.6 million as against the oil contribution of N8,880.8 million. This particular trend was maintained throughout the decades of the 1980s and early 1990s. However, with the introduction of value added tax in 1994, the relative importance of oil revenue began to reduce. In the first year of its introduction VAT contributed N7,260.8 million to the revenue. By 1998, the contribution of this non-oil revenue sub-head rose to N36,867.7, representing 8 per cent of all federally collected revenue and 21.2 per cent of non-oil revenue.

The issue of fiscal unitarism can best be appreciated by table 5. The table shows that between 1970 and 1980, the share of the federation account as a percentage of total federally collected revenue which was consistently over 90 per cent fell to 76.6 and 85.5 per cent, in 1981 and 1982, respectively. However, between 1983 and 1988, over 90 percentage points share was maintained. Thereafter, the share fluctuated between 74.9 per cent in 1991 and 35.7 per cent in 1997; but in 1998, the share stood at

55.5 per cent. On the average, the federal government retained about 93 per cent of public revenue annually between 1970 and 1998. This is a clear demonstration of a revenue imbalance between the various tiers of government in Nigeria. However, when this is juxtaposed with expenditure, the degree of expenditure imbalance was lower than revenue imbalance for most of the years. Indeed, the pattern of expenditure imbalance was fairly consistent during the review period (1970 and 1998). On aggregate, the states collected about 8.3 per cent of total revenue, while total expenditure hovered around 27.2 per cent on the average. This is indeed revealing, because the existing imbalance is essentially a product of the revenue allocation mechanism.

The level of dependence of the states and local governments for revenue could best be appreciated when the level of internally generated revenue of these levels of government are compared with the total revenue. For the states and the Federal Capital territory, this sources of revenue stood at 7.5 per cent during the same period. This level of imbalance is unacceptable. The other tiers of government (state and local) should be empowered to depend more on internally generated revenues so as to reduce the selective grant syndrome with all its attendant abuses that have bedevilled our revenue allocation mechanism under the military.

Under a democratic administration, there is the need to syste-matically devolve both the revenue raising and expenditure powers to the appropriate levels of government in order to make for stable polity. In this regard, the issue of refuse disposal which is local area specific, which has been left within the purview of the local government by the constitution, has not fared well. Perhaps not because of the level of government that is operating it, but probably due to the general inefficiency of government in business in Nigeria. There may be the need to privatise the refuse disposal system in Nigeria. It should be stated clearly here that the level of filth that our cities have been left in the past two decades is not acceptable in the civilized world of the 21st century.

However, as we have argued elsewhere, the capacity of government should be enhanced by adequate training on financial and other related management issues. It is our considered opinion that a reasonable level of education should be a requirement for occupying elective positions in Nigeria. This will have two major advantages: one, it will encourage people to go to school and thus reduce our illiteracy rate in the short run; and two, the people so educated will be equipped with the basic techniques of analysis so that every decision would be basically a product of informed analysis. We believe that there is a world of difference between incompetence and corruption. While the inability to properly situate and locate issues analytically may lead to wrong decisions and by extension wastage, the same cannot be said of the Chief Executive who is actually able to analyse the issue but prefers a sub-optimal choice because of personal gain. To my mind, the former is not corruption, but the latter is. Thus to confront corruption, which has been acknowledged, it is pertinent to confront the issue roundly. If the denial of public office to a certain group of people will act as an incentive to increase the literacy rate, and to a large extent, reduce wastage, we strongly recommend such a denial.

TABLE 1
Federation Account as a Percentage
of Federally-Collected Revenue

	Revenue	Federation Account	Federation Accounts as percentage of Federally-collected Revenue
1970	634	582.4	91.86
1971	116.8	1064.6	91.43
1972	1105.1	1325.8	94.36
1973	1695.3	1613	95.16
1974	4537.4	4371.0	96.33
1975	5514.7	5294.1	96.00
1976	6765.9	64070.1	95.62
1977	8042.2	7702.1	95.78
1978	7371.0	6781.4	92.00
1979	10912.4	10599.8	97.14
1980	15233.5	14746.5	96.80
1981	13290.5	10182.8	76.62
1982	11433.7	9884.9	86.45
1983	10508	9798.6	93.24
1984	11253.3	10672.4	94.84
1985	15050.4	13750.2	91.6
1986	12595.8	11868.3	92.1
1987	25380.6	24692.2	97.29
1988	27596.7	266770.3	97.10
1989	53870	46860.3	86.99
1990	98102	68064.2	96.38
1991	100991.6	756003.3	74.86
1992	190453.2	125255.7	65.77
1993	192769.4	131195.9	68.06
1994	201910.8	115698.2	57.30
1995	459987.3	170522.9	37.07
1996	520191.0	17000.0	34.41
1997	582811.1	20800.0	35.69
1998	463608.8	257.331.4	55.51

Sources: Central Bank of Nigeria, Statistical Bulletin, Vol 7 No 2 1992; and Annnual Report and Statement of Accounts for the year ended 31st December, 1996

TABLE 2
Sources of Revenue Governments in Nigeria (₦ Million)

Source	1990	1991	1992	1993
Federal Government				
Statutory Allocation from the Federation Account	23,575.0	19,742.2	38,240.0	51,797.7
Independent Revenue	1,724.0	3,040.4	4,903.1	5,626.5
Others (including Share of VAT, grants, etc)	12,853.1		10,121.0	68,647.0
Subtotal	38,152.1	30,829.2	53,264.1	126,071.2
Percentage of Total	65.6	55.4	62.0	68.0
State Government and FCT, Abuja)				
Statutory Allocation from the Federation Account	16,378.8	19,742.2	24,497.3	27,660.6
Internally generated Revenue	2,761.7	3,181.2	5,244.7	5,726.2
Others (including share of VAT, Grants, etc)	826.9	1,848.8	2,931.6	4,353.8
Subtotal	19,967.4	24,772.2	32,673.6	37,740.6
Percentage of Total	34.4	44.6	38.0	20.5
Local Government				
Statutory Allocation from the Federation Account	n.a.	n.a.	n.a.	18,316.4
Internally Generated Revenue	n.a.	n.a.	n.a.	1,035.6
Others (including share of VAT grants etc)	n.a.	n.a.	n.a.	522.5
Subtotal	n.a.	n.a.	n.a.	19,874.5
Percentage of Total	-	-	-	10.8
Grand Total for all Governments	58,119.5	55,601.4	85,937.7	183,686.3

79

TABLE 2
(Continued)

Source	1994	1995	1996	1997	1998
Federal Government					
Statutory Allocation from the Federation Account	53,661.0	78,569.3	81,056.0	101,000.0	124,572.9
Independent Revenue	3,888.2	20,761.0	3,407.0	8,339.3	3,447.8
Others (including Share of VAT, grants, etc)	33,073.7	150,437.8	240,681.0	241,922.4	182,158.3
Subtotal	90,622.9	279,768.1	325,144.0	351,262.3	310,174.0
Percentage of Total	56.9	73.0	74.1	73.5	62.5
State Government and FCT, Abuja)					
Statutory Allocation from the Federation Account	29,006.8	38,677.4	41,626.4	50,962.7	65,542.0
Internally generated Revenue	10,929.8	17,287.3	19,602.9	26,828.1	28,687.1
Others (including share of VAT, Grants, etc)	826.9	12,036.3	28,573.1	17,891.2	47,250.3
Subtotal	49,506.1	68,001.0	89,802.4	95,682.0	141,479.4
Percentage of Total	31.1	19.9	20.5	20.0	28.5
Local Government					
Statutory Allocation from the Federation Account	17,321.3	17,875.5	16,569.7	20,066.3	30,620.9
Internally Generated Revenue	1,205.9	2,110.8	2,027.1	2,515.6	3,331.6
Others (including share of VAT grants etc)	695.6	4,426.8	5,345.3	8,436.4	11,015.7
Subtotal	19,223.1	24,412.7	23942.1	31,018.3	44,968.2
Percentage of Total	12.1	7.1	5.5	6.5	9.0
Grand Total for all Governments	58,119.5	342,181.8	438,888.5	477,962.6	496,621.6

Sources: Derived from CBN Annual Report and Statement of Accounts (Various issues)

TABLE 3
Revenue and Expenditure of Government as a Percentage of GDP

Source	1990	1991	1992	1993	1994
Total Revenue N Million					
Federal Government	38,152.1	30,829.2	53,264.1	126,071.2	126,071.2
State Government	19,967.4	24,722.2	32,673.6	37,740.6	49,506.1
Local Governments	n.a.	n.a.	n.a.	19,874.5	19,233.1
Total Expenditure (N Million)					
Federal Government	60,268.2	66,584.4	92,797.4	191,228.9	160,893.2
State Governments	20,049.3	27,023.7	37,060.6	44,180.9	55.916.4
Local Governments	n.a.	n.a.	n.a.	19,475.7	18,967.1
Total Revenue	As Percentage of GDP				
Federal Government	14.6	9.5	9.7	18.1	9.9
State Government	7.6	7.6	5.9	5.4	5.4
Local Governents	n.a.	n.a.	n.a.	2.9	2.1
Total Expenditure	As Percentage of GDP				
Federal Governments	23.1	20.6	16.9	27.4	17.6
State Governments	7.7	8.3	6.7	6.3	6.1
Local Governments	n.a.	n.a.	n.a.	2.8	2.1
GDP at Current Market Prices (N bn)	260.6	324.0	549.8	697.1	914.9

**TABLE 3
(Continued)**

Source	1995	1996	1997	1998
Total Revenue N Million				
Federal Government	249,768.4	325,144.0	351,262.3	310,174.0
State Government	68,001.0	89,802.4	95,682.0	141,479.4
Local Governments	24,412.7	23,942.1	31,018.3	44,968.2
Total Expenditure (N Million)				
Federal Government	248,768.1	288,094.6	356,262.3	443,563.3
State Governments	79,591.6	84,177.1	92,647.6	138,452.2
Local Governments	22,443.3	24,261.7	30,833.0	42,741.2
Total Revenue	As Percentage of GDP			
Federal Government	12.6	11.5	12.0	10.9
State Government	3.4	3.2	3.3	5.0
Local Governents	1.2	0.8	1.0	1.6
Total Expenditure	As Percentage of GDP			
Federal Governments	12.6	10.2	12.1	15.6
State Governments	4.0	3.0	3.2	4.9
Local Governments	1.2	0.9	1.0	1.5
GDP at Current Market Prices (₦ bn)	1,977.7	2,823.9	2,939.5	2,837.2

Sources: Derived from CBN Annual Report and Statement of Accounts (Various issues)

TABLE 4
Sources of Revenue to State and Local Governments in Nigeria (₦ Million)

Source	1990	1991	1992	1993	1994
State Governments					
Statutory Allocation from Federation Account	16,378.8	19,742.2	24,497.3	27,660.6	29,006.8
Percentage of Total	82.0	79.7	75.0	73.3	58.6
Internally Generated Revenue	2,761.7	3,181.2	5,244.7	5,726.2	10,929.8
Percentage of Total	13.8	12.8	16.1	15.2	22.1
Others (including shares of Vat, grants etc)	826.9	1,848.8	2,931.6	4,353.8	9,569.5
Percentage of Total	4.1	7.5	9.0	11.5	19.3
Total for States	19,967.4	24,772.2	32,673.6	37,740.6	49,506.1
Local Governments					
Statutory Allocation from the Federation Account	n.a.	n.a.	n.a.	18,316.4	17,321.3
Percentage of Total	-	-	-	92.2	90.1
Internally Generated Revenue	n.a.	n.a.	n.a.	1,035.6	1,205.9
Percentage of Total	n.a.	n.a.	n.a.	5.2	6.3
Others (including shares of VAT, grants, etc)	n.a.	n.a.	n.a.	522.5	695.9
Percentage of Total for Local Governments	-	-	-	2.6	3.6
Total for Local Governments	-	-	-	19,874.5	19,223.1

TABLE 4
(Continued)

Source	1995	1996	1997	1998
State Governments				
Statutory Allocation from Federation Account	38,677.4	41,626.4	50,962.5	65,542.0
Percentage of Total	56.9	46.4	53.3	46.3
Internally Generated Revenue	17,287.3	19,602.9	26,828.1	28,287.1
Percentage of Total	25.4	21.8	28.0	20.0
Others (including shares of Vat, grants etc)	12,036.3	28,573.1	17,891.2	47,250.3
Percentage of Total	17.7	31.8	18.7	33.4
Total for States	68,001.0	89,822.4	95,682.0	141,479.4
Local Governments				
Statutory Allocation from the Federation Account	17,876.5	16,569.7	20,063.3	30,260.9
Percentage of Total	73.2	69.2	64.7	67.3
Internally Generated Revenue	2,110.8	2,027.1	2515.6	3,331.6
Percentage of Total	8.6	8.5	8.1	8.2
Others (including shares of VAT, grants, etc)	4,426.4	5,345.3	8,436.4	11,015.7
Percentage of Total for Local Governments	181.1	22.3	27.2	24.5
Total for Local Governments	24,412.7	32,942.1	31,018.3	44,968.2

Sources: Derived from CBN Annual Report and Statement of Accounts (Various issues)

TABLE 5
Central Revenue of the Federal Government(₦ Million)

Source	1970	1971	1972	1973	1974	1975	1976	1977	1978	1979
Total Federally Collected Revenue	634.0	1.168.8	1,405.1	1,695.3	4,537.4	5,514.7,	6,765.9	8,042.4	7,371.0	10,912.4
Oil Revenue	166.6	510.1	764.3	1,016.0	3,724.0	4,271.5	5,365.2	6,080.6	4,555.8	8,880.8
Petroleum Profit Tax	97.7	383.1	540.5	769.2	2,870.1	2,707.5	3,624.9	4,330.8	3,415.7	5,164.1
Others[2]	68.9	127.0	223.8	246.8	853.9	1,564.0	1,740.3	1,74908	1,140.1	3,716.7
Non-Oil Revenue	467.4	658.7	640.8	679.3	813.4	1,243.2	1,400.7	1,961.8	2,815.2	2,031.6
Company Income Tax	45.8	67.5	80.4	80.8	148.8	261.9	222.2	476.9	5,27.4	575.1
Customs & Excise Duties	370.0	491.0	481.1	516.2	498.3	760.7	882.7	1,145.6	1,698.2	1,143.9
Value Added Tax (VAT)	-	-	-	-	-	-	-	-	-	-
Federal Government Independent Revenue[3]	51.6	100.2	79.3	82.3	166.3	220.6	295.8	339.3	589.6	312.6
AFEM Surplus Revenue	-	-	-	--	-	-	-	-	-	-
Others[4]	-	-	-	-	-	-	-	-	-	-
Allocation To:	582.4	1,068.6	1,325.8	1,613.0	4,371.1	5,294.1	6,470.1	7,703.1	6,781.4	10,599.8
Federation Account	582.4	1,068.6	1,32538	1,613.0	4,371.1	5,294.1	6,470.1	7,7031	6,781.4	10,599.8
VAT Pool Account	-	-	-	-	-	-	-	-	-	-
AFEM Surplus Account	-	-	-	-	-	-	-	-	-	-
Petroleum Trust Fund	-	-	-	-	-	-	-	-	-	-
JVC Payments Account	-	-	-	-	-	-	-	-	-	-
External Debt Service Funds	-	-	-	-	-	-	-	-	-	-
National Priority Project Funds	-	-	-	-	-	-	-	-	-	-

TABLE 5
(Continued)

Source	1970	1971	1972	1973	1974	1975	1976	1977	1978	1979
Others[6]										
Federal Govt. Retained Revenue	448.4	1,168.8	1,404.8	1,695.3	4,537.0	5,514.7	6,765.9	8,042.4	5,178.1	8,868.4
Federation Account	397.2	1,068.6	1,325.5	1,613.0	4,370.5	5,294.1	6,470.1	7,703.1	4,588.5	8,555.8
Value Added Tax (VAT)	-	-	-	-	-	-	-	-	-	-
Federal Govt. Independent Revenue	51.6	100.2	79.3	82.3	166.3	220.6	295.8	339.3	589.6	312.6
PTF										
National Priority Projects										
External Debt Service Funds										
AFEM Surplus Intervention Fund										
Grant										
Others[7]										

TABLE 5
(Continued)

Source	1980	1981	1982	1983	1984	1985	1986	1987	1988	1989
Total Federally Collected Revenue	15,233.5	13,290.5	11,433.7	10,508.7	11,253.3	15,050.4	12,595.8	25,380.6	27,596.7	53,870.4
Oil Revenue	12,353.3	8,564.4	7,814.9	7,253.0	8,269.2	10,923.7	8,107.3	19,027.0	19,831.7	39,130.5
Petroleum Profit Tax	8,564.3	6,352.8	4,846.4	3,746.9	4,761.4	6,711.0	4,811.0	12,504.0	6,814.4	10,598.1
Others[2]	3,789.0	2,238.6	2,968.5	3,506.1	3,507.8	4,212.7	3,296.3	6,523.0	13,017.3	28,532.4
Non-Oil Revenue	2,880.2	4,726.1	3,618.8	3,255.7	2,984.1	4,126.7	4,488.5	6,353.6	7,765.0	14,739.9
Company Income Tax	579.2	403.0	550.0	561.5	787.2	1,004.3	1,102.5	1,235.2	1550.8	1,914.3
Customs & Excise Duties	1,813.5	2,325.8	2,336.0	1,984.1	1,616.0	2,183.5	1,728.2	3,540.8	5,672.0	5,815.5
Value Added Tax (VAT)	-	-	-	-	-	-	-	-	-	-
Federal Government Independent Revenue[3]	487.5	1,997.3	732.8	710.1	580.9	938.9s	433.7	407.6	540.5	938.0
AFEM Surplus Revenue	-	-	-	-	-	-	-	-	-	-
Others[4]	-	-	-	-	-	-	1,224.1	1,170.0	1.7	6,072.1
Allocation To:										
Federation Account	14,746.5	10,182.8	9,884.9	9,798.6	10,672.4	13,750.2	11,868.3	24,692.2	26,770.3	46,860.3
VAT Pool Account	14,746.5	10,182.8	9,884.8	9,798.6	10,672.4	13,750.2	11,868.3	24,692.2	26,770.3	46,860.3
AFEM Surplus Account	-	-	-	-	-	-	-	-	-	-
Petroleum Trust Fund	-	-	-	-	-	-	-	-	-	-
JVC Payments Account	-	-	-	-	-	-	-	-	-	-
ExternaDebt Service Funds	-	-	-	-	-	-	-	-	-	-
National Priority Project Funds	-	-	-	-	-	-	-	-	-	-

TABLE 5
(Continued)

Source	1980	1981	1982	1983	1984	1985	1986	1987	1988	1989
Others[6]	–	–	–	–	–	–	–	–	–	–
Federal Govt. Retained Revenue	12,993.3	7,511.6	5,819.1	6,272.0	7,267.2	10,001.4	7,969.4	16,129.0	15,588.6	25,893.6
Federation Account	12,505.8	5,514.3	5,086.3	5,561.9	6,686.3	9,062.5	6,311.6	14,551.4	15,046.4	18,752.1
Value Added Tax (VAT)	–	–	–	–	–	–	–	–	–	–
Federal Govt. Independent Revenue	487.5	1,997.3	732.8	710.1	580.9	938.9	433.7	407.6	540.5	938.0
PTF	–	–	–	–	–	–	–	–	–	–
National Priority Projects	–	–	–	–	–	–	–	–	–	–
External Debt Service Funds	–	–	–	–	–	–	–	–	–	–
AFEM Surplus Intervention Fund	–	–	–	–	–	–	–	–	–	–
Grant	–	–	–	–	–	–	1,224.1	1,170.0	–	–
Others[7]	–	–	–	–	–	–	–	–	1.7	6,072.1

88

TABLE 5
(Continued)

Source	1990	1991	1992	1993	1994	1995	1996	1997
Total Federally Collected Revenue	98,102.4	100,991.6	190,453.2	192,769.4	201,910.8	459,987.3	520,190.0	582,811.1
Oil Revenue	71,887.1	82,666.4	164,078.1	162,102.4	160,192.4	324,547.6	369,190.0	416,811.1
Petroleum Profit Tax	26,909.0	38,615.9	51,476.7	59,207.6	42,802.7	42,857.9	42,496.1	286,000.0
Others[2]	44,978.1	44,050.5	112,601.4	102,894.8	117,389.7	281,689.7	326,693.9	130,811.1
Non-Oil Revenue	26,215.3	18,325.2	26,375.1	30,667.0	41,718.4	135,439.7	151,000.0	166,000.0
Company Income Tax	2,997.3	3,827.9	5,417.2	9,554.1	12,274.8	21,878.3	22,000.0	26,000.0
Customs & Excise Duties	8,640.9	11,456.9	16,054.8	15,486.4	18,294.6	37,364.0	55,000.0	63,000.0
Value Added Tax (VAT)	-	-	-		7,260.8	20,761.0	31,000.0	34,000.0
Federal Government Independent Revenue[3]	1,724.0	3,040.4	4,903.1	5,626.5	3,888.2	20,436.4	3,407.0	8,339.9
AFEM Surplus Revenue	-	-	-	-	-	-	-	-
Others[4]	12,853.1	-	-	-	-	35,000.0	39,593.0	34,660.1
Allocation To:	84,735.4	76,350.9	126,486.4	162,746.4	194,362.7	439,226.3	517,190.0	578,568.6
Federation Account	68,064.2	54,000.0	77,800.0	106,799.4	115,698.2	170,522.9	179,000.0	208,000.0
VAT Pool Account	-	-	-	-	7,260.8	20,436.4	31,000.0	34,000.0
AFEM Surplus Account	-	-	-	-	-	79,645.3	103,190.0	130,811.1
Petroleum Trust Fund	-	-	-	-	9,957.5	35,000.0	42,000.0	37,757.5
JVC Payments Account	16,671.2	22,350.9	48,686.4	55,947.0	61,446.2	45,000.0	39,000.0	45,000.0
External Debt Service Funds	-	-	-	-	-	44,000.0	44,000.0	44,000.0
National Priority Project Funds	-	-	-	-	-	26,000.0	44,000.0	44,000.0

89

TABLE 5
(Continued)

Source	1990	1991	1992	1993	1994	1995	1996	1997
Others[6]	-	-	-	-	-	18,621.7	35,000.0	35,000.0
Federal Govt. Retained Revenue	38,152.1	30,829.2	53,264.9	126,071.2	90,622.6	249,768.1	325,144.0	351,262.3
Federation Account	23,575.0	27,788.8	38,240.0	51,797.7	53,661.0	325,144.0	81,056.0	101,000.0
Value Added Tax (VAT)	-	-	-	-	1,452.2	7,437.8	10,746.0	12,238.7
FederalGovt.Independent Revenue	1,724.0	3,040.4	4,903.1	5,626.5	3,888.2	20,761.0	3,407.0	8,339.9
PTF						35,000.0	41,935.0	37,757.5
National Priority Projects	-	-	-	55,947.0	19,826.4	26,000.0	44,000.0	44,000.0
External Debt Service Funds	-	-	-	-	-	44,000.0	41,285.2	32,924.1
AFEM Surplus Intervention Fund	-	-	-	-	-	38,000.0	62,000.0	47,002.1
Grant	-	-	-	-	-		2,000.0	2,000.0
Others[7]	12,853.1	-	10,121.8	12,700.0	11,794.8	-	38,714.8	66,000.0

1 Revised
2 Includes revenue from export sales, royalties, rent etc.
3 Comprises revenue from interest payments rents on Government Properties, Personal
  Income Tax of Armed Forces, Police, External Affairs, and Federal Capital Residents
4 Includes Customs Levies and Education Taxes etc
5 Includes transfers to Federation Account from Domestic Oil Sales
6 Includes transfers to Speical and Excess Reserves, Education Fund
7 Includes Draw-down from Fertiliser Reserve, Customs Levies, Subvention/Grants, and Sterilised Oil Windfall Proceeds and
  Sterilised Oil Windfall Proceeds and Grants

Sources: (1) Federal Ministry of Finance and Economic Development
         (2) Central Bank of Nigeria

Chapter Eight

Evaluation of the Revenue Allocation Criteria

There are two fundamental issues that have always arisen with respect to revenue sharing in any federation. The fiirst is how inequalities in size and wealth between units affect fiscal relations between governments. In all federations there are relatively rich and relatively poor units of government. While the poor are often favoured and struggle for what has been called a redistributive system of federal finance, the rich on the other hand are often more interested in autonomy in revenue allocation which is based on the relative contributions of each unit to the federal purse. The second issue is the extent to which transfer of revenue between governments can be used to promote political stability and even development. From the analysis, we shall see how these problems have been minimised.

From the presentation of the various formulae, it could be seen that there are two ways of sharing revenue in a federation. These are the vertical and horizontal allocations. The vertical allocation has to do with the percentage of revenue given to the different tiers of government and that allotted to the special fund, while the horizontal allocation takes care of the allocation among the states and local governments and the statutory grants given to the states and the respective weights given to the various principles. It could be seen that there have been considerable changes in the vertical allocation of revenue. In 1989, the federal government allocation was 55 per cent while the states and local governments settled for 32.3 per cent and 10 per cent, respectively. This did not allow for enough decentralization of funds for all the levels of government. To this end, there has been a general concern about the manner in which funds are disbursed from the Federal Account to states and local governments.

It could be seen from the data presented above that the states seem to be forced to go cap in hand to the federal government begging for funds. The condition of the second tier of government (the State) seems to be worse off as their allocation continually, decreases, rather than increase. The most recent revenue allocation formula attests to this.

Presently, state Governors everywhere are complaining about this situation. The Governors are of the view that the present revenue allocation formula has left them with inadequate funds to fulfil their campaign promises to the populace. Before now, when the local government fund was not paid directly to the Local Government Joint Account, the State Governments were alleged to have routinely diverted the funds meant for their local governments leaving the local governments chronically short of funds. This widespread practice frustrated local governments from embarking on meaningful development projects and, thereby, stifled grassroot development.

However, the allocation to local governments seem to be really appreciating. This tier has been encouraged and equipped to play its role as the third tier of government whose activities impinge directly on the welfare of the rural masses. Though there have been frequent relocations of fiscal powers among the three tiers of government, there has been no power to the states in the collection of revenue from their areas of jurisdiction. Therefore, in the final analysis, the state still suffers more than all other tiers (Federal and Local Governments). There has been an element of politics in this vertical allocation of revenue, but from a closer look, successive administrations have reduced it to a considerable extent. The Federal Government allocation reduced from 55 per cent in 1989 to 48.5 per cent in 1992, while the local governments had an increase in allocation, from 10 per cent in 1989 to 20 per cent in 1992. The state, all the same, is still left cap in hand, begging for more money to carry out its projects.

Considering the horizontal allocation made so far, it could be seen that emphasis is mostly placed on the following criteria: equality, population; social development factor; landmass; internal revenue effort. Equality still maintains its weight of 40 per cent, thereby, showing that all the States in the federation are given the same percentage of funds to aid even development. Population before now was given 40 per cent weight but has been reduced to 30 per cent, the recent formula proposes 25.0 per cent. This has serious implications. Much effort was put in by the respective states to increase their population figures and make things more difficult in economic planning and management. During Babangida's administration, the social development factors decreased from 15 per cent in 1989 to 10 per cent in 1992 and these factors included education, health and water. All these were in a bid to reach out to as much as possible, the populace, and encourage manpower development in Nigeria. As in 1989, landmass and terrain were not given any weight but because of continuous lobbying by States that have a vast landmass, and thus feel they are not properly developed, there has been a weight attached to it - 10 per cent. The other principle is the Internal Revenue Effort which has to do with the funds given to the States as a result of whatever they have been able to generate internally.

The last to be considered is the Special Fund which in 1989 stood at 5 per cent but which during the1992 revenue allocation formula was increased to 7.5 per cent. From here, derivation which turns out to be the most controversial issue in the criteria for revenue sharing was raised from 1.5 per cent to 3 per cent. However the 1999 constitution assigned a weight of at least 13.0 per cent to this factor.

From the foregoing analysis, it could be seen that the much talked about politics in revenue allocation is in the areas of population, derivation, on-shore and off-shore dichotomy. Population, though a good factor in any federal system for allocation of revenue, has been unduly emphasized. Even with the recent population figure of Nigeria there are still doubts about the accuracy of the figures. Most ethnic groups still feel that their population has a lot to do in revenue sharing matters as much revenue has been given to more populous states. But the reduction in the weight by 10 per cent has not done enough. The weight now stands at 25 per cent.

The issue of on-shore and off-shore oil dichotomy as it applied to the derivation principle is another serious bone of contention in revenue sharing in Nigeria. This was introduced by the Dina Commission of 1969. The Okigbo Commission of 1980 retained it and it still holds now. This practice, it is generally believed, is politically tainted, prejudiced and biased and deliberately designed to deprive the minority oil- producing areas of a fair and equitable share of national resources. Also, it is seen as an indication that the majority ethnic groups are prepared to adopt all possible strategies to alienate and relegate the minority oil - producing states to the background. The plight of the minority oil -producing areas have been so deplorable that oil -producing communities have been reduced to penury following the combined activities of oil prospecting and extracting companies.

Derivation in the actual sense until recently was 1.5 per cent of the 5 per cent special fund. Although the belief in some quarters is that the 1.5 per cent allocated for the development of oil -producing areas was adequate and should even be reviewed downwards, a greater number argued that the percentage allocated to this factor was inadequate and should be revised upwards, in view of the ecological disasters that have often befallen these areas whose sources of livelihood, especially, agriculture and fishing, have been wiped out by pollution resulting from oil exploitation. The very deplorable condition of all the oil -producing communities throughout the country attests to this fact. However, the Babangida administration changed the weight assigned to the development of the oil- producing areas. The percentage of revenue given to the oil- producing states was increased by 100 per cent, that is from 1.5 per cent to 3 per cent. However, the 1999 constitution of the Federal Republic of Nigeria pegged the derivation at,at least,13.0 per cent.

The Obasanjo administration have in their short stay in office identified the shortcomings of the revenue allocation formula, especially as it relates to the development of the oil- producing areas. In this direction, the President presented a Bill on the Niger-Delta Development Commission{ NNDC) Act to the   National Assembly within the first few months of the Administration. This is indeed very commendable, however, the selection process should ensure that only people with proven integrity are allowed to serve on the Commission. In addition, the leadership of the Commission should be the exclusive preserve of the Niger-Delta States. There should be a provision in the Act when amended to ensure that the commission is held accountable for the formulation of a development plan for the Niger-Delta. In this direction, a comprehensive development programme that will take into account the peculiar needs of the region should be drawn up. The plan should specify explicitly the number of roads, schools, hospitals and other social infrastructures that will be provided on a yearly basis. The National Assembly should be brought in to scrutinise the

Commission's progress. The Boards should be given yearly targets, and the failure to meet the targets should be considered as a lack of competence. In addition, apart from the political office in the Commission, the technical staffing should be depoliticised so as to attract competent and qualified personnel from any part of the country or beyond. The NNDC Act is included as Appendix I.

Chapter Nine

Offshore/Onshore Oil Dichotomy: Emerging Issues

Before 1914 and up till 1960, Nigeria was colonized by Britain. In order to maximize the material benefits of the resources found in her territory, all manners of laws and policies were promulgated and enforced without any regard to the feelings or the welfare of the natives. One of such laws was the Mineral Ordinance Act of 1945 promulgated by the British Colonial Office. The ordinance stipulated that "the entire property and control of all mineral oil, in, under, or upon any land in Nigeria, and of all rivers, streams, and water courses throughout Nigeria, is and shall be vested in the crown" where the crown meant British Colonial Government.

In 1960, when Nigeria became an independent state, the Founding Fathers in their wisdom, drastically altered this obnoxious and colonial ordinance. Indeed, the 1963 constitution was fashioned in such a way that derivation as a principle of revenue allocation was assigned at least 50.0 per cent. This arrangement was, however, altered during the Military regime of Gowon 1966-1975. Indeed, during this regime, political   exigency necessitated the creation of additional states from the former three regions to bring the total number of states in the country to twelve. On the economic front, oil was discovered and suddenly became the mainstay of the economy. In early 1970s, the military regime of Gowon abolished the 50 per cent derivation policy entrenched in the 1963 Constitution and   enacted what most commentators have come to refer to as villainous Decree 9 of 1971. The decree states that "the rights of the regions to the minerals in their continental shelves are abrogated and ownership and title to the territorial waters, continental shelf as well as royalties, rents and other revenue derived there-from or relating to the operation, prospecting or searching or winning or working of petroleum from seaward appurtenances of the states are vested in the Federal Government".

A cursory perusal of the decree reveals a repackage of the 1945 British Colonial Mineral Ordinance. To further strengthen the Federal Government's grip on the natural resources, the Obasanjo Military regime in 1976 promulgated the land use decree. Indeed, through various decrees and manipulations of the political and economic powers by the successive military regimes in Nigeria, the percentage allocation for derivation has declined from over 50 per cent in the early 1960s to just 3.0 per cent in 1999 and13 per cent in 2001. In addition to this drastic reduction came the onshore - offshore dichotomy.

The Babaginda Military Administration abolished the onshore-offshore dichotomy in 1992. Before the advent of democracy in Nigeria in 1999, the federal government did not take the dichotomy into consideration in giving states their allocation, although only three per cent was assigned to derivation.

Given the constitutional provisions of at least 13 per cent to derivation (1999 Constitution), the states requested the federal government to implement the provision of the Constitution as it affects revenue allocation. But the federal government objected, claiming she was awaiting the Revenue Mobilization and Fiscal Commission to submit its report on the sharing of the nation's revenue. However, the government continued to assign 3.0 per cent to derivation. Expectedly the affected states objected to the federal government decision and agitated for more revenue based on the 1999 Constitutional provisions.

As a result of increasing agitation for natural resources control, by some states of the federation (mostly oil producing states), the Federal Government on February 6, 2001 instituted a law suit at the Supreme Court seeking the interpretation of the apex court of the constitutional provision for the control and management of the nation's natural resources. The suit number SC28/2001 was filed in response to the claims of the littoral states namely; Akwa Ibom, Bayelsa, Cross River, Delta, Edo, Ogun, Ondo and Rivers States, that the natural resources located offshore ought to be treated or regarded as located within their respective states.

The Federal Government in the said suit prayed the court to determine the seaward boundary of littoral states within the Federal Republic of Nigeria; for purpose of calculating the amount of revenue accruing to the Federal Account directly from any natural resources derived from that state pursuant to section 162 (2) of the 1999 Constitution. The Government contended that the seaward boundary of each of the said states is the low water mark of the land surface or the seaward limits of inland waters within the state. Therefore, the natural resources found within the territorial waters of Nigeria and the Fedcral Capital Territory are derived from the federation and not from any state. The Federal Government also argued that the natural resources located within the Exclusive Economic Zone and the continental shelf of Nigeria are subject to provisions of any treaty or other agreement between Nigeria and any neighbouring littoral foreign state. The full text of the statement of claims is annexed to the Book as (Appendix II).

Section 162 (1-4) of the 1999 Constitution of the Federal Republic of Nigeria states that: 162-

(1)   The Federation shall maintain a special account to be called "The Federation Account" into which shall be paid all revenue collected by the Government of the Federation, except the proceeds from the personal income tax of the personnel of the Armed Forces of the Federation, the Nigeria Police Force, the Ministry or department of government charged with responsibility for Foreign Affairs and the residents of the Federal Capital Territory, Abuja.

(2)   The President, upon the receipt of advice from the Revenue Mobilization Allocation and Fiscal Commission, shall table before the National Assembly proposals for revenue allocation from the Federation Account, and in determining the formula, the National Assembly shall take into account the allocation principles especially those of population, equality of States, internal revenue generation, land mass, terrain as well as population density.

Provided that the principle of derivation shall be constantly reflected in any approved formula as being not less than thirteen per cent of the revenue accruing to the Federation Account directly from any natural resources.

(3)   Any amount standing to the credit of the Federation Account shall be distributed among the

*Federal and State Governments and local govern-
ment councils in each State on such terms and in
such manner as may be prescribed by the National
Assembly.*

*(4)   Any amount standing to the credit of the
States in the Federation Accounts shall be distributed among the States on such terms and in such
manner as may be prescribed by the National
Assembly.*

I am not a lawyer, consequently, my contribution here is not to
be construed as a legal opinion neither is this volume seeking to
join issues in the case. Having said that, a cursory perusal of the
above constitutional provisions for revenue sharing had not made
any provision for the offshore/onshore dichotomy that the
Federal Government has been trying to introduce into the
sharing of oil revenue in Nigeria. Admittedly, these distinctions
were made from the 1970s to early 1990s. However, the
Babangida administration abolished the offshore/onshore
dichotomy in 1992. It is therefore not clear why the PDP
Government has held tenaciously onto the non-existent principle
for the purpose of revenue allocation to the affected states. For
record purposes, the Federal Government had tried thrice to
officialise the offshore/onshore oil dichotomy. The first was in
the year 2000 appropriation bill, second, in the NDDC bill and
finally in the year 2001 appropriation bill. In all these instances,
the National   Assembly removed the dichotomy before passing
the relevant Bills. Indeed, section 313 stipulates that the system of
revenue allocation in existence for the financial year beginning
from 1st   January, 1998 and ending at 31st December 1998 shall
continue to apply pending any Act of the National Assembly for
such provisions between the Federal and the States and Local
Government Councils and among Local Government Councils
in the States. Empirically, the derivation principles as

implemented by the government today guarantee 60 per cent of the 13 per cent stipulated in the constitution denying the oil producing states their legitimate revenue.

The Nigerian Constitution made provision for only one federal capital territory, Abuja. There is no law that established the body of water that surrounds Nigeria as a federal capital territory, thus oil that accrues from these waters which forms part of the states cannot directly accrue to the Federal Government.

In conclusion, it might be proper to take a critical look at the constitutional provisions regarding power of both the state and federal government in terms of resource control. Whatever, the outcome of the recent court case, one thing is clear; over-concentration of power over natural resources at the federal level in Nigeria does not augur well for fiscal federalism.

The worst that can happen to Nigeria's federalism is for any unit especially, the minorities to be made to feel that they are being penalized, marginalized or cheated just because they are minorities. (See Appendix III for the initial ruling on the case between the Federal Government and the States).

Chapter Ten

Options and Challenges*

The imperatives for revenue transfer from higher to lower tiers of government in a federation include:

(I)   The need for "balancing of deficiency" transfers, necessitated by imbalances between revenues and responsibilities;

(II)   Equalization transfer, necessitated by variations in the revenue raising capacities of the lower level government such that heavier tax burdens in the lower levels are eliminated; and

(III)   "Stimulation" incentives or "Promotion" transfers which are regarded as functional or conditional, in that they are made with specific instructions as to their disbursement and utilization.

The grant system, which is in recognition of both budgetary obligation and largely dependent on needs of the States and Local Governments, enables the Federal Government to transfer financial resources to the former. The issue however, is that the grant system has been arbitrary and unpredictable, while the basis of allocation is subjected to underhand political, and personal pressures and arrangements. Also, hand in hand with the expansion of federal grants has been federal control. Most often federal officials and federally funded projects in States and Local Governments usurp the functions of these levels of government.

The 1999 Constitution bestowed the power to impose tax on the Federal Government ,while it also bestowed the collection and utilization of tax proceeds in respect of personal income and duties on the states. The constitution is however, silent on the role of Local Governments in matters of tax jurisdiction. The Federal Government is responsible for the collection of revenue sources that go into the Federation Account. These are mainly indirect (PPT, companies income tax, and capital gains tax); Customs and Excise (i.e. export, import and excise) duties and fees, and mining, namely, oil pipelines licence fees, rent on mineral licence, royalty on oil and gas, NNPC earnings from the direct sale of crude oil for domestic consumption, and penalty for gas flaring.

The Federal Government's independent revenue is made up of direct taxes such as personal income tax on members of the armed forces, police, external affairs officers, as well as residents of the FCT. These sources, in addition to those listed earlier constitute the inter-governmental revenue sources. They include both tax-based revenues and those realized from user-charges.

The 1999 Constitution in conferring a lot of tax jurisdiction on the Federal Government has also perpetuated the conditions making for the lower level's dependence on the centre and for dependence on revenues based on statutory allocations. The latter accounts for at least 60 per cent of the total revenue of the most financially viable state.

Additionally, the structure of allocated revenues has always been lopsided. At first revenues from import and export duties dominated, and now these have been replaced by earnings from the oil sector that form the bulk (up to 90 per cent) of allocated revenues. The generally poor tax base of federal fiscal revenues, especially non-oil sources makes revenue generation at the federal level erratic and unpredictable. Actual revenues are dependent on volatile market and political circumstances. Revenue expenditure and planning are therefore unstable, while depen-dence on a single revenue source affects the overall economic viability and capacity to sustain a diversified and rich revenue resource base.

The heavy dependence on Federal revenue sources has led to the emergence of a fiscal imbalance between the Federal Government on one hand, and the States and Local Governments, on the other. States have experienced budget deficits while the Federal Government has enjoyed budget surpluses. This was especially true of the decades of the 1970s-1980s. One major cause of a declining proportion of federal revenue going to the States and Local Governments is that the most buoyant federal revenue sources (e.g. Petroleum Profit Tax) were not within the revenue allocation formula.

This heavy dependence on statutory allocation is revealed by the proportion of such revenue to the total revenue resources available to the states and local governments. When a state realizes up to 80 per cent of its recurrent revenues through the revenue allocation system, and about 2/3 of this is from one revenue source (oil), the fiscal position with its overall recurrent revenue structure is certainly lopsided and precarious. A depression in the markets for oil will thus plunge the whole federal finances into difficulties, making it impossible for governments to meet their obligations or even plan properly. The national average dependency ratio for states is about 75 per cent and this is very much higher for the Local Governments.

The paucity of the States' own sources of revenue in comparison with their expenditure is indicated by the fact that, on average, in the years 1976-80 ,states incurred 47.7 per cent of recurrent public sector expenditure, but received directly only 6.5 per cent of public sector tax revenues (Onwioduokit, 1998). If any lessons are to be drawn from the foregoing discussions, one such lesson is that revenue trends in the next millennium will be significantly affected by the mechanisms of socio-economic and political reform measures put in place by government. While the larger essence of the reforms is to rationalize the public and private sectors of the economy, the focus on governmental operations also indicates an emphasis on rationalizing governmental responsibilities in the light of fiscal realities.

Thus, in addition to new types of fiscal jurisdiction delineation and resource allocation, there will be further need to minimize further conflicts and lack of coherence in the fiscal network of relations between and among the interacting levels of government. There will also be the need for clearer fiscal policies that are both equitable and efficient, stable as well as supportive of the principles of fiscal federalism.

Expenditure levels by each tier of government will be significantly affected by the cost factor within the national economy as well as inflation, which could raise the cost of such items as public medicare, building materials, education, infrastructure, fertilizer, etc. Already, the federal government has been searching for a suitable system of deregulation and subsidy withdrawal. Thus, a machinery is already in place to ensure that in the face of cost overruns, the responsibilities of government are rationalised in more efficient resources utilization and managerial capacities.

Yet, it is to be expected that the traditional expenditure items of government would remain stable, and should be so in order to guarantee a minimum acceptable level of socio-economic development and national integration. In fact, under the current economic downturn, many more people will come to depend on public sector expenditure and budgetary allocations both for welfare and capital formation needs. It is therefore, reasonable to assume that, all things being equal, there is going to be noticeable government revenue shortfalls in relation to governmental expenditure requirements.

The tendency for government expenditures to outpace revenue is termed the fiscal crisis of the state. The propensity to spend more than we are prepared to finance through taxes is becoming deep seated and ominous. Numerous government programmes have a huge growth of expenditures built into them. It is precisely due to this reason that one finds a large number of stalled or uncompleted projects spanning all the three tiers of government. Expenditure at all levels of government reveals an increasing trend in all categories, yet effective service delivery and the current state of socio-economic infrastructure are not encouraging. These require the injection of either finance capital in respect of socio-economic infrastructure or human resources development programmes to boost skill and efficiency in the public service. There is also an urgent need for change in both the attitude to work in the public sector as well as the plugging of the loopholes in revenue resources management and utilization.

There is, of course, no iron law that expenditure must not always rise more rapidly than revenue, but it is a fact also that growing needs which only the government can meet create even greater claims on the budget. Several factors may offset the fiscal crisis:

a)   People who need government-provided services may be ignored and their needs neglected; either through cut backs, ability to pay/afford clauses, or the reduction of public sector subsidies as in privatization and commercialization programmes;

107

b) Corporations that depend on public revenue in the form of loans, grants or subsidies may not get them;

c) Public sector employees' income may fall below private sector income;

d) People can be made to pay higher taxes, or (if unwilling) indirectly by financing increased public expenditures via inflation credit expansion.

A combination of some of these measures has already been adopted in our Structural Adjustment Programme; but the issue of tax politics is very new to Nigeria. For example, who will pay for rising government expenditure? Would some areas of public spending rise while others are cut? Can the government deliver more and better service for less taxes? Can the fiscal systems survive its present forms? All these are questions requiring political and economic solutions.

But the concerns of fiscal policies are the discovery of the principles governing the volume and allocation of public finances and expenditures as well as the distribution of the tax burden among them. The example of the local governments' finances in relation to their new roles are used to illustrate this point. It is also well to remember that the volume and composition of government expenditure and the distribution of the tax burden are not determined by market forces, but rather by the socio-political and economic relations that characterize inter-governmental fiscal relations. No one is exempt from the fiscal crisis and the underlying social crises that it aggravates.

Thus, the limited fiscal capacity of all the governments necessitates a critical look at the adequacy of their tax base(s). This limited capacity in absolute and relative terms is goal-jeopardizing in every important respect. The proportion of company income tax in the total tax revenue (federally-collected) is very small. Yet the current depreciation of the Naira and the high cost of foreign exchange have together accounted for a drop in indus-trial capacity utilization and therefore a low tax base.

Some of the issues and challenges that appear to dominate Revenue Allocation in Nigeria today and how the resolution of these issues would affect future developments are presented below:

- One key issue is the nature of our political economy. Currently, over 90 percent of all accruable federally-collected and shared revenue comes from a single commodity, crude oil. The dominance of oil in the structure, size, sharing determinants, flow stability of resources and domestic politics has created a very unhealthy development in Nigeria's fiscal federalism and development challenges.

- Issues such as the incessant dissatisfaction and communinity tension especially among and within the oil-producing communities has risen to the level where such communities in their feeling of alienation, have resorted to direct attacks on oil installations, corpora-tions and bloody communal clashes.

- The dominance of oil has led to the illusion, in which the nation has assumed an adequate or unlimited flow of resources. This illusory approach has led to the axiomatic situation in which the non-oil sector has been neglected and its contribution to revenue resources has been declining proportionately.

- There is the absence of both forward and backward inte-gration of the oil sector and the monetized oil revenues in diversifying the national economic base.

- The dominance of oil has also raised the issue of disequilibrium in which the political and economic

109

relations within the federation are seen in discordant ways with the oil-producing communities clamouring for a better share of the resources tapped from their territories, in addition to the provision of basic infrastructure. The reference here is the old regional arrangement in which derivation played a dominant role in resource allocation, and/or allowed regions to retain a large chunk of revenues generated within the regions.

- The oil phenomenon must thus be revisited and ascertained as to whether or not it can be equated to the old economic base of regional marketing and Commodity Boards. The sovereign and national (Federal) claims to legal ownership of all mineral resources is therefore in question. These issues constitute one of the major challenges of future fiscal relations in Nigeria.

- The military factor in Nigerian politics, and the regimentation of society as well as the relations which shape intergovernmental relations, has also led to the centralization of public policy with the lower tiers being reduced to simply toeing the line or implementing policies and directives from the centre. The identification of this military factor, aquires even more significance if it is examined within the challenges which are already being publicly expressed.

- The democratization of the society and the location or linking of fiscal policy formulation to popular participation and collaboration between the legislature and the executive arm, should reduce the tendency for unilateral executive decisions.

- Inter - governmental relations (IGR) should evolve procedural, more objective and fairly acceptable policies if they are subjected to inter - governmental policy and agency consultation, coordination and democratic decision - making.

- The lack of a complete census aimed at identifying the full mineral and other resources, their spatial and quantita tive (as well as qualitative) distribution, should be given priority consideration. A strategic policy of the exploitation, marketing, utilization or monetisation (overall development) can then be mapped out.This is essential so that every component of the federation is given equal opportunity to develop and make a contribution to the resource base of the nation. In this regard, initial resources should be shared between the various tiers of government according to their absorptive capacity. This will reduce the current feelings of some sections which are seen as being 'parasitic'. This is both an issue of equity as well as a strategic management challenge.

- Ideally, any allocation formula should at the same time be an instrument o f resource mobilization. It is crucial therefore that rather than consume what we produce, the allocation formula contains within it parameters for savings and investments abroad, in safe portfolios and politically - friendly nations. This shock - absorbing mechanism has proved very useful in raising the quantum of revenue flows, giving the national average in international relations as well as serving as fall-back base in cases of emergency or disaster.

111

- The institutionalization of savings meant for investment both within and outside the country entails that a credible body made up of eminent and competent Nigerians, who would serve as the Board of Trustees, for the management of such funds, is necessary. This body should administer the funds after a careful, and thorough cost-benefit assessment of options. Similarly, such a body should develop a stable long-term, medium and short-term policy guidelines which are to be implemented irrespective of regime type(s) or character(s).

- There should also be the development of modalities and strategies for the empowerment of communities and political/administrative units to develop new resource bases and more efficient accountability and probity measures in resource utilization. For example, such units should be allowed access to the money, capital and investment markets/sectors for sourcing funds for public projects. This can easily be done through the securitization of both their nominal allocations in both the suspense and Federation Account as well as Stabilization Accounts.

- The disequilibrium in resources flow where some tiers of government record financial surpluses in the face of deficits at other tiers further compounds the fiscal crisis the nation is going through. T his leads to intensified lobbying of the Executive for special grants, or where States and Local Governments have to compete for access and influence peddling in order to secure adequate/additional funds.

- The size of the Special Funds (Accounts) may be broadened to include investments in Research and Development (R & D), technological advances and the development of socio-economic infrastructure.

112

- As much as possible, policies with additional expenditure burdens should not be unilaterally imposed on any tier of government in order to avoid fiscal indiscipline, deficits and political crisis. This is especially so with policies that are introduced midstream in the fiscal year, such as the 1993 and the 1998 Federal Government salary increases which nearly paralyzed the lower tiers of government.

- There may be the need for the re - examination of the constitutionally - assigned roles, responsibilities and functions of all tiers of government and to realign these with both resource availability and a new concept of federalism which emphasizes shared responsiblities rather than separation. This is not to be misconstrued as an assault on the principles of Federalism, but rather developing relevant and appropriate principles commensurate with our history, politics, obstacles, challenges and their capacity - building factor for overcoming developmental challenges.

- The establishment of legislative and public accountability guidelines for all revenue generating, collectin and utilization agencies. This should be coupled with an adequate and effective (applicable) sanction and reward system. The system of executive exemptions extended to powerful persons and interest groups, which are selective and unfair, and lead to institutional drift in revenue management and fiscal controls should also be stopped.

- The de-politicizing and de - emotionalizing of issues through the use of an ad hoc fire-fighting approach in place of permanent, credible agencies, that can be independently funded and run so that the issue of revenue allocation is not seen to be influenced by only a single tier of government.

Selected References

Adedeji, A. 1969. "Revenue Allocation in Nigeria" *Financial Journal: 5 (1)*

Amucheazi, E.C. (Ed.). 1998. *Reading in Social Sciences: Issue in National Development*, Enugu: Fourth Dimension.

Ashwe, Chichi.1986. *Fiscal Federation in Nigeria*. Canberra, Australia National University.

Awa, E.O. 1976. *Issues in Federation*, Benin City: Ethiope Publishing House.

Awa, E.O. 1994. Federal Government in Nigeria.

Brennan, Geoffrey, and James, M.B. 1998. *The Power to Tax: Analytical Foundations of Fiscal Constitution*, New York: Cambridge University Press.

Cremer, Jacques, Antonio, E. and Paul, S. 1994. "The Decentralization of Public Services: Lessons from the Theory of the Firm" *Policy Research Working Paper 1345.* Office of the Vice-President, Development Economics, World Bank, Washington, DC.

Ekpo, A. H. 1999. "Federation and Local Government Finances in Nigeria" in *Fiscal Federalism and Nigeria's Economic Development*, Nigerian Economic Society, Ibadan.

Ekpo, A. H. and J.E.U. Ndebbio 1998. *Local Government Fiscal Operations in Nigeria.* AERC Research paper No.73, March.

Ekpo, A. H. 1994. "Fiscal Federalism: Nigeria's Post-Independence Experience, 1960-90. *World Development*, Vol. 22, No. 8 pp 1129-1146.

Elaigwu, J. I. Et al (eds). 1994. *Federations of Nigerian Federalism.* Vol. 3

Elaigwu J. I. Et al (eds). 1994. Federation and National Building in Nigeria.

Faruquee, R. 1994. Nigeria: Ownership Abandoned in Adjustment in Africa, Word Bank.

Friedrich, Carl. 1964. *Trends in Federalism in Theory & Practice.*

Ida, I. M. 1994. Revenue Allocation in Nigeria Today: Issues and Challenges. *An address to the Committee on Revenue Allocation of the National Constitutional Conference.*

Musgrave, R.A. and Musgrave, P.B. 1984. Public Finance. Theory and Practice, New York: Mc GrawHill.

Oates, Wallace E. 1972. Fiscal Federalism, New York: Harcourt, Brace, Jocanovich.

1994. "The Potential and Perils of Fiscal Decentralization". University of Maryland, Department of Economics, College Park.

Onazi, O.C. 1999. Welcome Address at the Conference on New Direction in Federation in Africa, Abuja March.

Onwioduokit, E.A. 1998. "Local Government Viability: Unsettled Issues" processed.

Onwioduokit, E.A. 1998. Governance and Economic Development in Nigeria, *CBN Occasional Paper Series* (processed)

Oyovbaire, S.E. 1985. Federalism in Nigeria.

1995a. "Basic Issues of Decentralization and the Tax Assignment". In Ehtsham Ahmad, Gao Qiang, and Vito Tanzi, eds., Reforming China's Public Finances, Washington, D.C.: International Monetary Fund.

Philip, A . 1991. "Managing Fiscal Federalism: Revenue Allocation Issues" Publius, Vol. 21 (4) pp. 103-112.

Pruo' homone, Remy. 1959. "On the Dangers of Decentralisation". World Bank Research Observer 10 (2): 201-20.

Shah, Anwar, and Zia Qureshi . 1994. Intergovernmental Fiscal Relations in Indonesia: Issues and reforms Options. World Bank Discussion Paper 239. Washington D.C.

Rampahl, S. 1976. Keynote Address at the International Conference on Federalism. N.I.I.A. Lagos, May.

Tanzi, Vito. 1994. "Corruption, Governmental Activities and Markets" IMF Working Paper 94/99. International Monetary Fund, Washington, D.C.

Thisday Newspaper. 2001. Various Issues

Tiebout, C.M. 1956. "A Pure Theory of Local Expenditures." Journal of Political Economy 5 (October): 416-24.

Ukpong, I.I. 1984. Notes on Nigeria's Fiscal Policy, Uyo: Oduduma.

Wheare, K.C. 1964. Federal Government.

APPENDIX I

A Bill
For

An Act to Establish the Niger-Delta Development Commission 1999
Arrangement of Sections

Section
Part I - Establishment, etc; The Niger-Delta Development Commission and the Governing Council.

Establishment of the Niger-Delta Development Commission etc.

Establishment of the Niger-Delta Development Commission

Tenure of Office of Council Members

Rotation of Office of Chairman of the Commission

Cessation of Membership of the Council, etc

Allowance of Members

Part II - Functions and Powers of the Commission, etc

Functions and Powers of the Commission

Powers of the Council

Part III - Structure of the Commission

Establishment of directorates

Establishment of the Management Committee

Establishment of the Niger-Delta Development Advisory Committee

Part IV - Staff

Application of Managing Director, etc.

Service in the Commission to be pensionable.

Part V - Financial Provisions

Fund of the Commission

Expenditure

Gifts to the Commission

Powers to borrow

Annual estimates and expenditure

Quarterly Report

Annual Report

Part VI - Miscellanous

Establishment of Monitoring Committee

Offices and premises of the Commission

Directives by the President, Commander-in-Chief of the Armed Forces.

Limitation of suit against the Commission, etc

Service of Documents.

Restriction on Execution against property of the Commission

Indemnity of Officers

Repeal of 1998 No 41, and savings, provisions etc.

Regulations

Interpretation

Citation

Schedule

Preamble

A bill for an Act to provide for the repeal of the Oil Mineral Producing Areas

Commission decree 1998, and among other things, establish a new Commision with a re-organised management and administrative structure for more effectiveness; and for the use of the sums received from the allocation of the Federation Account for tackling ecological problems which arise from the exploration of oil minerals in the Niger-Delta area.

Part 1 - Establishment of The Niger-Delta Development Commission and the Governing Council

1-(1) There is hereby established a body to be known as Niger-Delta Development Commission (in this Act referred to as "the Commission").

The Commission -

(a) shall be a body corporate with perpetual succession and common seal;

(b) may sue and be sued in its corporate name. The Commission shall have its head office in Port Harcourt,River State and shall establish an office in each member State of the Commission.

2 (1)   There is hereby established for the Commission a governing Council (in this Act referred to as "Council"), which shall consist of -

(a) a Chairman;

(b) one person who shall be an indigene to represent each of the following member States, that is:-

(i)   Abia State

(ii) Akwa-Ibon State

(iii) Bayelsa State

(iv) Cross River State

(v)   Delta State

(vi) Edo State.

(vii) Imo State

(viii) Ondo State, and

(ix) River State

(c)   two persons to represent non-oil pro-
        ducing States

(d)   one representative of oil-producing
        companies in the Niger- Delta to be
        nominated by the oil-producing
        companies;

(e)   one person to represent the Federal
        Ministry of Finance;

(f)   the Marketing Director of the Com-
        mission

3.   The Chairman and other members of the Coun-
        cil shall -

(a)   be appointed by the President, Com-
        mander-in-Chief of the Armed Forces,
        and

(b)   be persons of proven integrity and
        ability.

(c)   the members of the Council referred
        to in paragraph

(d)   Sub-section (i) of the section shall
        be part-time members.

The supplementary provisions set out in the Schedule to
this Act shall have effect with respect to the proceedings of
the Council and other matters contained therein

3 (1) Subject to the provision of section 4 of this Act a
member of the Council, other than an ex-officio member,
shall hold office for a term of 4 years at the first instance
and may be re-appointed for a further term of 4 years
and no more.

2. The members of the Council shall be paid such remunerations and allowances as the Federal Government may, from time to time, determine for the Chairman and members of statutory boards generally.

3. A member of the Council other than an ex-officio member may resign his appointment by notice, in writing under his hand addressed to the President, Commander-in-Chief of the Armed Forces, which resignation shall take effect only on acknowledgement by the President, Commander-in-Chief of the Armed Forces.

1999 No. C 48

4. The Office of Chairman of the Commission shall rotate among the member States of the Commission in the following alphabetical sequence-

    (a)   Abia State;

    (b)   Akwa-Ibom State;

    (c)   Bayelsa State;

    (d)   Cross River State;

    (e)   Delta State;

    (f)   Edo State;

    (g)   Imo State;

    (h)   Ondo State; and

    (i)   Rivers State;

5. (1) Notwithstanding the provisions of section 3 of this Act, a person shall cease to hold office as a member of the Council if

    (a)   he becomes bankrupt, suspends payment of compounds with his creditors; or

    (b)   he is convicted of a felony or any offence involving dishonesty or fraud; or

    (c)   he becomes of unsound mind, or incapable of carrying out his duties; or

(d) he is guilty of a serious misconduct in relation to his duties; or

(e) in the case of a person dispossessed of professional qualifications, he is dis-qualified or suspended, other than at his own request, from practising his pro-fession in any part of the world by an order of a comptent authority made in respect of that member; or

(f) he resigns his appointment by a letter addressed to the President, Commander-in-Chief of the Armed Forces.

(2) A member of the Council may be removed by the Presi-dent, Commander - in - Chief of the Armed Forces, if he is satisfied that it is not in the interest of the Commission or the interest of the public that the member should continue in office.

(3) Where a vacancy occurs in the membership of the Coun-cil, it shall be filled by the appointment of a successor to hold office for the remainder of the term of office of his predeces-sor, so however, that   the successor shall represent the same interest and shall be appointed by the President, Commander-in-Chief of the Armed Forces.

6. There shall be paid to every member of the Council such allowances and expenses as the Federal Government may, from time to time, determine.

Part II - Functions and Powers of the Commis-sion etc

7.(1) The Commission shall -

(a) formulate policies and guidelines for the development of the Niger-Delta area;

(b) conceive, plan, and implement, in ac-cordance with set rules and regulations, projects and programmes for the deve-lopment of the Niger-Delta area in the

124

field of transportation including roads, jetties and waterways, health, and education, industrialization, agriculture and fisheries and urban development, water supply, electricity and telecommunications;

(c) cause the Niger-Delta area to be surveyed in order to ascertain measures which are necessary to promote its physical development;

(d) prepare schemes designed to promote the physical development of the Niger-Delta area and the estimates of the costs of implementing such schemes.

(e) implement all the measures approved for the development of the Niger-Delta area by the Federal Government and the member States of the Commission;

(f) identify factors inhibiting the development of the Niger-Delta area and assist the member States in the formation and implementation of policies to ensure sound and efficient management of the resources of the Niger-Delta area;

(g) assess and report on any project being funded or carried out in the Niger-Delta area by oil - producing companies and any other company including non - governmental organizations and ensure that funds released for such projects are properly utilized;

(h) tackle ecological problems that arise from the exploration of oil mineral in the Niger - Delta area and advise the Federal Government and the member states on the prevention and control of oil spillages and environmental pollution;

(i) liaise with the various oil mineral prospecting companies in all matters of pollution prevention and control;

(j)   execute such other works and perform such other functions which , in the opinion of the Commission, are required for the development of the Niger - Delta area and its people; and

(k)   carry out such other functions as the President may , from time to time , direct.

(2) In exercising its functions and powers under this section, the Commission shall have regard to the varied and specific contributions of each member State of the Commission.

(3) The Commission shall not be subject to the direction, control or supervision of any other authority or person in the performance of its function under this Act other than the President, Commander-in-Chief of the Armed Forces.

8.-The Council shall have power to:

(a)   manage and superintend the affairs of the Commission;

(b)   make rules and regulations for carrying out the functions of the Commission;

(c)   enter and inspect premises, projects and such places as may be necessary for the purposes of carrying out its functions under this Act;

(d)   pay the staff of the Commission such remuneration and allowances as are payable to persons of equivalent grades in the civil service of the Federation;

(e)   enter into such contracts as may be necessary or expedient for the discharge of its functions and ensure the efficient performance of the functions of the Commission;

(f)   do such other things as are necessary and expedient for the efficient performance of of the functions of the Commission.

126

PART III - Structure of the Commission

9(1) There shall be established in the head office of the
Commission, the following Directorates-

(a)   the Directorate of Administration
and Personnnel Management;

(b)   the Directorate of Community and
Rural Development;

(c)   the Directorate of Infrastructural
Development;

(d)   the Directorate of Environmental Protection;

(e)   the Directorate of Finance and
Supply;

(f)   the Directorate of Agriculture, Fisheries and Water Supply;

(g)   the Directorate of Planning, Research
and Statistics;

(h)   the Directorate of Legal Services.

(2)   The Council may, with the approval of the
President, Commander-in Chief of the Armed
Forces, increase the number of Directorates as
it may deem necessary and expedient to facili-
tate the realization of the objectives of the Commission

10. There shall be for the Commission, a Management Committee which shall-

(a)   consist of a Chairman who shall
be the Managing Director , the
Directors responsible for the Directorates established under section 9 of
this Act and such number or other
members as may be determined from
time to time;

(b)   be responsible to the Council and the Managing Director of the general administration of the Commission.

11.(1) There is hereby established for the Commission, a Niger-Delta Development Advisory Committee (in this Act referred to as "the Advisory Committee) which shall consist of -

    (a)   the Governors of the member States of the Commission; and

    (b)   such other persons as may be determined, from time to time, by the President, Commander-in-Chief of the Armed Forces.

(2) The Advisory Committee, shall be charged with the responsibility of advising the Council and guiding and monitoring the activities of the Commission with a view to achieving the objectives of the Commission.

(3) The Advisory Committee may make rules regulating its own proceedings.

Part IV - Staff

12.(1) There shall be for the Commission, a Managing Director, who shall -

    (a)   be an indigene of one of the member States of the Commission;

    (b)   not be below the rank of a Permanent Secretary in the civil service of the Federation;

    (c)   have such qualification and experience as are appropriate for a person required to perform the functions of that office under this Act; and

    (d)   be the Chief Executive and accounting officer of the Commission;

    (e)   be appointed by the President, Com-

mander - in - Chief of the Armed
Forces;

(f)   hold office on such terms and conditions as to emolument, conditions of
service as may be specified in his
letter of appointment.

(2)The Managing Director shall, subject to the general
direction of the Council, be responsible

(a)   for the day to day administration of the
Commission;

(b)   for keeping the books and proper
records of the proceedings of the
Council; and

(c) for-

(i) the administration of the secre-
tariat of the Council and

(ii) the general direction of the Council subject to the directives of
the Council and the Chairman.

(3) The Council shall have power to-

(a)   employ either directly or on second-
ment from any civil or public service
in the Federation or a State such
number of employees as may, in the
opinion of the Council, be required to
assist the Council in the discharge of
any of its functions under this Act; and

(b)   pay to persons so employed such
remuneration (including allowances)
as the Council may, after consultation
with the Federal Civil Service Commission, determine.

13.(1) Service in the Commission shall be approved service
for the purpose of the pension Act.

(2) The officers and other persons employed in the Commission shall be entitled to pensions, gratuities and
other retirement benefits as are enjoyed by persons

the   holding equivalent grades in the civil service of
                    Federation.

(3)   Nothing in sub-sections (1) and (2) of this section
                    shall prevent the appointment of a person to
                    any office or terms which preclude the grant
                    of pension and gratuity in respect of that office.

(4)   For the purpose of the application of the provi-
                    sions of the Pensions Act, any power exerci-
                    sable thereunder by the Minister or other autho-
                    rity of the Government of the Federation, other
                    than the power to make regulations under sec-
                    tion 23 thereof; is hereby vested in and shall be
                    exercisable by the Commission, and not by any
                    other person or authority

Part V - Financial Provisions

14.(1)The Commission shall establish and maintain a fund
    from which shall be defrayed all expenditure incurred
    by the Commission.

    (2) These shall be paid and credited to the fund established
    pursuant to subsection (1) of this section-

        (a)   from the Federal Government , the
                    equivalent of 10 per cent of the total
                    monthly statutory allocations due to
                    member states of the Commision from
                    the federation account;

        (b)   50 per cent of the 13 per cent of the
                    revenue accruing to the Federation
                    Account under sub-section (2) of sec-
                    tion 162 of the Constitution of the
                    Federal Republic of Nigeria 1999,
                    deductible at source;

        (c)   per cent of the total annual budget of
                    any oil producing company operating,
                    on shore, in the Niger-Delta area;

        (d)   50 per cent of monies due to member
                    States of the commission from the Eco-
                    logical Fund;

(e)   such monies as may from time to time, be granted or lent to or deposited with the Commission by the Federal or a State Government, any other body or institution whether local or foreign;

(f)   all moneys raised for the purposes of the Commission by way of gifts, loans, grants-in-aid, testamentary dispositions or otherwise; and

(g)   proceeds from all other assets that may, from time to time, accrue to the Commission.

(3) The fund shall be managed in accordance with the rules made by the Council, and without prejudice to the generality of the power to make rules under this subsection, the rules shall in particular contain provisions-

(a)   specifying the manner in which the assets or the fund of the Commission are to be held, and regulating the making of payments out of the fund; and

(b)   requiring the keeping of proper accounts and records for the purpose of the funds in such form as may be specified in the rules.

15 - The Commission shall apply the proceeds of the fund established pursuant to section 14 of this Act to-

(a)   the cost of administration of the Commission;

(b)   the payment of salaries, fees, remuneration, allowances, pensions, gratuities payable to the members of the Council specified in section 6 of this Act or any committee of the Council and the employees of the Commission;

(c)   the payment for all contracts, including mobilization, fluctuations, variations, legal fees and cost on contract administration;

(d)   the payment for all purchases, and

(e)   undertaking such other activities as
        are connected with all or any of the
        functions of the Commission under
        this Act

16 (1) The Commission may accept gifts of land, money or
       other property on such terms and conditions, if any, as
       may be specified by the person or organization
       making the gift.

   (2) The Commission shall not accept any gift if the condi-
       tions attached by the person or organization making
       the gift are inconsistent with the functions of the Com-
       mission under this Act

17 The Commission may, with the consent of the President,
   Commander-in-Chief of the Armed Forces, borrow on
   such terms and conditions as the Commission may determine, such sums of money as the Commission may
   require in the exercise of its functions under this Act.

18 (1) The Council shall not later than 30th September each
       year, submit to the President, Commander-in-Chief
       of the Armed Forces, an estimate of the expenditure
       and income of the Commission in the succeeding year.

   (2) The Council shall cause to be kept proper accounts of
       the Commission in respect of each year and proper
       records in relation thereto and shall cause the Accounts
       to be audited not later than 6 months after the end of
       each year by auditors appointed from the list and in
       accordance with the guidelines supplied by the
       Auditor-General for the Federation.

19 - The Commission shall, at the end of every quarter in
     each year, submit to the President, Commander-in-Chief
     of the Armed Forces, a report on the activities and
     administration of the Commission.

20 (1) The Council shall prepare and submit to the President,
       Commander- in -Chief of the Armed Forces, not later
       than June in each year, a report in such form as the
       President, Commander-in -Chief of the Armed Forces,
       may direct on the activities of the Commission during
       the immediately preceding year, and shall include in
       the report a copy of the audited accounts of the Com-
       mission for that year and the auditor's report thereon.

(2) The President, Commander-in-Chief of theArmed Forces shall, upon receipt of the report referred to in sub-section (1) of this section, cause a copy of the report and the audited accounts of the Commission and the auditor's report thereon to be submitted to each House of the National Assembly.

Part VI - Miscellaneous

21.(1) There is hereby established for the Commission a Monitoring Committee which shall consist of such number of persons as the President, Commander-in-Chief of the Armed Forces, may deem fit to appoint from the public or civil service of the Federation.

(2) the Monitoring Committee shall -

(a) monitor the management of the funds of the Commission and the imple-mentation of the projects of the Com-mission , and

(b) have access to the books of account and other records of the Commission at all times , and submit periodical reports to the President, Commander-in-Chief of the Armed Forces.

22.(1) For the purposes of providing offices and premises necessary for the performance of its functions under this Act, the Commission may, subject to the Land Use Act

(a) purchase or take on lease any interest in land, or other property; and

(b) construct offices and premises and equip and maintain same.

(2) The Commission may, subject to the Land Use Act, sell or lease out any office or premises held by it, which office or premises is no longer required for the performance of its functions under the Act.

23 - Subject to the provisions of this Act; the President, Com-mander-in -Chief of the Armed Forces, may give to the Commission directives of a general nature or relating generally to matters of policy with regard to the

peformance by the Commission of its functions and it shall be the duty of the Commission to comply with the directives.

24.(1)Subject to the provisions of this Act, Offices Protection Act shall apply in relation to any suit instituted against any officer or employee of the Commission.

(2)Notwithstanding anything contained in any other law or enactment, no suit shall lie against any member of the Council, the Managing Director or any other officer or employee of the Commission for any act done in pursuance or execution of this Act or any other law or enactment, or of any public duty or authority or in respect of any alleged neglect or default in the execution of this Act or such law or enactment, duty authority, shall lie or be instituted in any court unless-

(a)   it is commenced within three months next after the Act, neglect or default complained of; or

(b)   in the case of a continuation of damage or injury, within six months next after the ceasing thereof.

(3) No suit shall be commenced against a member of the Council, the Managing Director, officer or employee of the Commission before the expiration of a period of one month after written notice of intention to commence the suit shall have been served upon the Commission by the intending plaintiff or his agent.

(4) The notice referred to in subsection (3) of this section shall clearly and explicitly state the cause of action, the particulars of the claim, the name and place of abode of the intending plaintiff and the relief which he claims.

25.-A notice, summons or other document required or authorised to be served upon the Commission under the provisions of this Act or any other law or enactment may be served by delivering it to the Managing Director or sending it by registered post and addressed to the Managing Director at the principal office of the Commission.

26.-(1) In any action or suit against the Commission, no execution or attachment of process in the nature thereof shall be issued against the Commission.

134

(2) Any sum of money which may by the judgement of any court be awarded against the Commission shall, subject to any direction given by court where notice of appeal of the said judgement has been given, be paid from the general reserve fund of the Commission.

27- A member of the Council, the Managing Director, or any officer or employee of the Commission shall be indemnified out of the assets of the Commission against any proceeding, whether civil or criminal , in which judgement is given in his favour, or in which he is acquitted, if any such proceeding is brought against him in his capacity as a member of the Council , the Managing Director, officer or employee of the Commission.

28- (1) The Oil Mineral Producing Areas Development Commission Decree 1998 is hereby repealed and accordingly the Commission established under the Decree (in this section referred to as "the dissolved Commission") is consequently dissolved.

(2) By virtue of this Act, there shall be vested in the Commission immediately at the commencement of this Act, without further assurance, all assets, funds, resources and other movable and immovable property which immediately before the commencement of this Act, were vested in the dissolved Commission.

(3) As from the date of commencement of this Act-

(a) all rights, interests, obligations and liabilities of the dissolved Commission existing before the commencement of this Act under any contract or instrument, or in law or in equity, shall by virtue of this Act be assigned to and vested in the Commission

(b) any contract or instrument as is mentioned in paragraph (a) of this subsection shall be of the same force and effect against or in favour of the Commission established by this Act and shall be enforceable as fully and effectively as if instead of the dissolved Commission, the Commission had been named therein or had been a party thereto;

(c) the Commission shall be subject to all the obligations and liabilities to which the dissolved Commission was subject immediately before the commencement of this Act and all other persons shall have the same rights, powers and remedies against the Commission as they had against the dissolved Commission immediately before the commencement of this Act.

(4) Any proceedings or cause of action pending or existing immediately before the commencement of this Act or against the dissolved Commission in respect of any right, interest, obligations or liability of the dissolved Commission may be commenced or continued, as the case may be, and any determination of any court of law, tribunal or other authority or person may be enforced by or against the Commission to the same extent that the proceedings, cause of action or determination might have been continued, commenced or enforced by or against the dissolved Commission as if this Act had not been made.

(5) Notwithstanding the provisions of this Act but subject to such directions as may be issued by the Commission, a person who immediately before the commencement of this Act held office in the dissolved Commisssion shall be deemed to have been transferred to the Commission on terms and conditions not less favourable than those obtaining immediately before the commencement of this Act, and service in the dissolved Commission shall be deemed to be service in the Commission for purposes of pension

(6) The President, Commander-in-Chief of the Armed Forces, if he thinks fit may, within twelve months after the commencement of this Act, by order published in the Gazette, make additional transitional or saving provisions for the better carrying out of the objectives of this section.

29 The Commission may, with the approval of the President, Commander-in-Chief of the Armed Forces, make regulations, generally for the purposes of giving full effect to this Act.

30 In this Act, unless the context otherwise requires, "Chair-man" means the Chairman of the Council."Commission" means the Niger - Delta Development Commission established by section 1 of this Act;

"Council" means the governing Council established for the Commission under section 2 (1) of this Act

"Member" means a member of the Council and includes the Chairman.

"Member Sates" includes Abia, Akwa - Ibom, Bayelsa, Cross River, Delta, Edo, Imo, Ondo and River State.

31 This Act may be cited as the Niger-Delta Development Commission (Establishment etc) Act 1999.

Schedule   Section 2 (4)

Supplementary Provisions Relating to the Council, etc.

Proceedings of the Council

1-   (1)Subject to this Act and Section 27 of the Interpretation Act the Council may make standing orders regulating its proceedings or those of any of its committees.

(2)The quorum of the Council shall be the Chairman or the person presiding at the meeting and 4 other members of the Council, and the quorum of any committee of the Commission shall be as determined by the Council.

2 -   (1) The Council shall meet whenever it is summoned by the Chairman and if the Chairman is required to do so by notice given to him by not less than 4 other members, he shall summon a meeting of the Council to be held within 14 days from the date on which the notice is given.

(2) At any meeting of the Council, the Chairman shall preside but if he is absent, the members present at the meeting shall appoint one of their number to preside at the meeting.

(3) Where the Council desires to obtain the advice of any person on a particular matter, the Council may co-opt him to the Council for such period as it deems fit,but a person who is in attendance by virtue of this sub-paragraph shall not be entitled to vote at any meeting of the Council and shall not count towards a quorum.

COMMITTEES

3.-   (1) The Council may appoint one or more committees to carry out, on behalf of the Council, such
functions as the Council may determine.

(2) A committee appointed under this paragraph
shall consist of such number of persons that may be
determined by the Council and a person shall hold
office on the committee in accordance with the
terms of his appointment.

(3) A decision of a committee of the Council shall be
of no effect until it is confirmed by the Council.

1. Miscellaneous

4.   (1) The fixing of the seal of the Commission shall
be authenticated by the signatures of the Chairman or any other member of the Council generally or specifically authorized by the Council
to act for that purpose and the Managing
Director.

(2) Any contract or instrument which, if made
or executed by a person not being a body corporate, would be required to be under seal and may
be made or executed on behalf of the Commission by the Managing Director or any person
generally or specifically authorized by the Council to act for that purpose.

(3) A document purporting to be a document duly
executed under the seal of the Commission shall
be received in evidence and shall, unless and
until the contrary is proved, be presumed to be
so executed.

5.   The validity of any proceedings of the Council
or of a committee shall not be adversely affected by

(a)   a vacancy in the membership of the
Council or committee; or
(b)   a defect in the appointment of a member
of the Council or committee
(c)   reason that a person not entitled to do so
took part in the proceedings of the Coucil
or Committee.

138

MADE at Abuja this day of 1999
OLUSEGUN OBASANJO, GCFR,
PRESIDENT COMMANDER-IN-CHIEF of the Armed
Forces,
Federal Republic of Nigeria

APPENDIX II

Resource Control Suit:
FG's Statement of Claims Details of the suit
filed by the Federal Government against the
36 states on February 6

1.   The Plaintiff is the Attorney-General of the
Federation and brings this action as the representative of the
Government of the Federal Republic of Nigeria.

2.   The first to the 36th defendants (states) are the
attorneys-general of each of the 36 states which along
with the   Federal Capital Territory, Abuja comprise the
Federal Repu-blic of Nigeria. Each defendant is sued as the
representative of the government of each state.

3.   Section 162 (1) of the Constitution of the Federal
Republic of Nigeria, 1999 (hereafter referred to as "the
Constitution") provides that the federation shall maintain
a special account to be called "the Federation Account"
into which shall be paid all revenue subject to certain exceptions which are not material to this case collected by
the federation.

4.   Pursuant to the provisions in Section 162 (2) of
the Constitution and subject to certain conditions therein
specified, the President of the Federal Republic of Nigeria
is required to table before the National Assembly proposals
for revenue allocation.

5.   By a proviso to the aforementioned Section 162
(2) of the Constitution, the principle of derivation must be
reflected in any approved formula for revenue allocation.

6.   The plaintiff states that in the context of Section
162 (2) of the Constitution the expression "principle of
derivation" means the principle that revenue accruing to
the Federation Account from any natural resources shall

be deemed to have been derived from the state or territory where such resources are   located.

7.   The plaintiff further states that the proviso to Section 162 (2) of the Constitution requires that any approved formula for revenue allocation from the Federation Account shall reflect the fact that not less than 13 per cent of revenue accruing to the said Federation Account from any natural resources are allocated to the government of the state or territory where such resources are located.

8.   By reason of the fact pleaded in paragraphs 5, 6 and 7 of this statement of claim, the Plaintiff states that for the purpose of calculating the amount of revenue accruing to the Federation Account directly from any natural resources derived from any state or territory pursuant to the proviso to Section 162 of the Constitution:

a)   The natural resources located within the boundaries of any state are deemed to be derived from that state

b)   In the case of the littoral states comprised in the Federal Republic of Nigeria (i.e. the states of Akwa-Ibom, Bayelsa, Cross Rivers Delta, Lagos, Ogun, Ondo, and Rivers) the sea-ward boundary for each of the said states is the low water mark of the land surface thereof or (if the case so requires) the seaward limits of inland waters within the state;

c)   The natural resources located within the territorial waters of Nigeria and the Federal Capital Territory are deemed to be derived from the federation and not from any state.

d)   The natural resources located within the exclusive economic zones and the continental shelf of Nigeria are subject to the provisions of any treaty or other written agreement between Nigeria and any neighbouring littoral foreign state, derived from the federation and not from any state.

9.   In further support of the averments on paragraph 8 of this statement of claim the Plaintiff will contend at the trial of this action that under the provisions contained in the Constitution it is only the Federal Government of Nigeria and not the government of any of the states comprised in the Federal Republic of Nigeria that has power to:

(i) exercise legislative, executive, or judicial powers over the entire area designated as the "territorial waters of Nigeria" pursuant to the provisions of the Territorial Waters Act, Cap. 428, Laws of the Federation of Nigeria 1990, as amended,

(ii) exercise any of the sovereign rights exercisable by Nigeria over the entire area designated as the "Exclusive Economic Zone" pursuant to the provisions of the Exclusive Economic Zone Act, Cap. 110, Laws of the Federation of Nigeria, as amended.

10.   The States of Akwa-Ibom, Bayelsa, Cross River, Delta, Edo, Ogun, Ondo and Rivers despite the averment of the Federal Government of Nigeria as pleaded in paragraph 8 hereof claim that natural resources located offshore ought to be treated or regarded as located within their respective states.

Whereupon the plaintiff claims:

A determination by this honourable court of the seaward boundary of a littoral state within the Federal Republic of Nigeria for the purpose of calculating the amount of revenue accruing to the Federation Account directly from any natural resources derived from that state pursuant to the proviso to Section 162 (2) of the Constitution of the Federal Republic of Nigeria, 1999.

APPENDIX III

'There is Dispute Between FG, Littoral States'

Being the lead ruling of the Chief Justice of the Federation, Justice Mohammed Uwais in the objections of 11 states to the onshore/offshore suit filed by the Federal Government.

Pursuant to the provisions of Order 3 Rule 3 of the Supreme Court Rules, 1985, the Attorney-General of the Federation filed a Statement of Claim in this Court in order to commence proceedings in the original jurisdiction of this Court under section 232 of the Constitution of the Federal Republic 1999, against the thirty six Attorneys-General of all the States of the Federal Republic of Nigeria. The Statement of Claim avers as follows:-

1.   The Plaintiff is the Attorney-General of the Federation and brings this action as the representative of the government of the Federal Republic of Nigeria.

2.   The 1st to the 36th Defendants are the Attorneys-General of each of the 36 states which along with the Federal Capital Territory Abuja, comprise the Federal Republic of Nigeria. Each defendant is sued as the representative of the Government of each State.

3.   Section 162 (1) of the Constitution of the Federal Republic of Nigeria, 1999 (hereafter referred to as "the Constitution") provides that the Federation shall maintain a special account to be called "the Federation Account" into which shall be paid all revenue subject to certain exceptions which are not material to this case collected by the Federation.

4.   Pursuant to the provisions in Section 162 (2) of the Constitution and subject to certain conditions herein specified, the President of the Federal Republic of Nigeria is required to table before the National Assembly proposals for revenue allocation.

5.   By a proviso to the aforementioned Section 162 (2) of the Constitution, the principle of derivation must be reflected in any approval formula for revenue allocation.

6.   The Plaintiff states that in the context of Section 162 (2) of the Constitution the expression "principle of derivation" means the principle that revenue accruing to the Federation Account from any natural resources shall be deemed to have been derived from the State or territory where such resources are located.

7.   The Plaintiff further states that the proviso to Section 162 (2) of the Constitution requires that any approved formula for revenue allocation from the Federation Account shall reflect the fact that not less than 13 per cent of revenue accruing to the said Federation Account from any natural resources are allocated to the Government of the State or territory where such resources are located.

8.   By reason of the facts pleaded in paragraphs 5,6 and 7 of this Statement of Claim, the Plaintiff states that for the purpose of calculating the amount of revenue accruing to the Federation Account directly from any natural resources derived from any State or territory pursuant to the proviso to Section 162 of the Constitution.

(a)   The natural resources located within the Boundaries of any State are deemed to be derived from that State;

(b)   In the case of the littoral States comprised in the Federal Republic of Nigeria (i.e. the States of Akwa-Ibom, Bayelsa, Cross River, Delta, Lagos, Ogun, Ondo and Rivers) the Seaward Boundary of each of the said States is the low water mark of the land surface thereof or (if the case so requires) the seaward limits of   inland waters within the State;

(c)   The natural resources located within the territorial Waters of Nigeria and the Federal Capital Territory are deemed to be derived from the Federation and not from any State;

(d)   The natural resources located within the Exclusive Economic Zone and the Continental Shelf of Nigeria are subject to the provisions of any treaty or other written   agreement between Nigeria and any neighbouring littoral foreign State, derived from the Federation and not from any State.

9.   In further support of the averments in paragraph 8 of this Statement of Claim, the Plaintiff will contend at the trial of this action that under the provisions contained in the Constitution it is only the Federal Government of Nigeria and not the Government of any of the States com-

143

prised in the Federal Republic of Nigeria that has power to:-

(i)   exercise legislative, executive, or judicial powers over the entire area designated as the "territorial waters of Nigeria" pursuant to the provisions of the Territorial Waters Act, Cap. 428, Laws of the Federation of Nigeria 1990, as amended;

(ii)   exercise any of the sovereign rights exercisable by Nigeria over the entire area designed as the "Exclusive Economic Zone pursuant to the provisions of the Exclusive Economic Zone Act, Cap. 110, Laws of the Federation of Nigeria, as Amended.

10.   The States of Akwa-Ibom, Bayelsa, Cross River, Delta, Lagos, Ogun, Ondo and Rivers dispute the averment of the Federal Government of Nigeria as pleaded in paragraph 8 hereof and claim the natural resources located offshore ought to be treated or regarded as located within their respective States.

WHEREUPON the Plaintiff claims:-

A determination by the Honourable Court of the seaward boundary of a Littoral State within the Federal Republic of Nigeria for the purpose of calculating the amount of revenue accruing to the Federation Account directly from any natural resources derived from the State pursuant to the proviso to Section 162 (2) of the Constitution of the Federal Republic of Nigeria, 1999. All the defendants except the 29th and 30th have filed Statements of Defence. Eleven out of 36 Defendants have raised preliminary objections in their Statements of Defence challenging the jurisdiction of this Court to hear the suit. These are the 1st, 3rd, 4th, 6th, 9th, 10th, 11th, 28th and 32nd defendants. The grounds of the preliminary objections varied. They however include the following:-

(1)   That the suit is academic, frivolous, vexatious and speculative;

(2)   That the non-littoral States are not parties to the suit and ought to be struck out.

(3)   That the original jurisdiction conferred on the Supreme Court does not extend to the realm of International Law;

(4)   That the Supreme Court has no jurisdiction to entertain the Plaintiff's claim or grant the reliefs sought as the Constitution vests the power upon the National Assembly only to determine the formula for revenue allocation including allocation on the basis of the principle of derivation;

144

(5)   That the plaintiff's claim for the Supreme Court to determine the boundary of the littoral States is not justifiable since the Court has no jurisdiction to determine State boundaries.

(6)   That the plaintiff's action does not disclose a reasonable cause of action.

(7)   The plaintiff's claim does not establish the existence of a valid dispute whether of law or fact; nor disclose the existence or extent of a legal right.

(8)   That the plaintiff lacks the locus standi to bring the action ;

(9)   That the suit raises political questions and is an abuse of the judicial process;

(10)   That the action is not properly constituted and is incurably defective on grounds of misjoinder of non-littoral States in the suit;

(11) That the Supreme Court lacks the jurisdiction to grant the relief sought and to interprete section 162 subsection (2) of the Constitution including the proviso thereof:-

(12)   That the action is premature as the President of the Federal Republic of Nigeria has not yet tabled any proposal for revenue allocation before the National Assembly in accordance with section 162 subsection (2) of the Constitution;

(13)   That the delimitation, demarcation or adjustment of boundaries between States is the responsibility of the Executive or the Legislature;

(14) That it is proper for the plaintiff to start the action by filing a Statement of Claim instead of issuing an originating summons;

(15) That there is no legislation the interpretation of which will enable the Supreme Court to determine the seaward boundary of littoral States; and

(16) That any determination of the seaward boundary of a Littoral State is tantamount to the Supreme Court delimiting the international maritime boundary of the Federal Republic of Nigeria, which is beyond the juridical competence of the Court.

On the 9th April 2001 when the case came up for mention, we directed the parties to each file a brief of argument in respect of the grounds of their preliminary objection and the plaintiff to file one brief of argument in reply to all the eleven defendants' briefs. This has been done. At the hearing of the objections, all the parties adopted the arguments in their briefs. With the exception of the 4th and 12th defendants, learned counsel also argued orally in expatiation of the briefs.

I intend to deal with all the grounds of objection under the following headings:-

JURISDICTION

Learned counsel for the eleven defendants have argued that the provisions of section 232 of the Constitution of the Federal Republic of Nigeria 1999 (hereinafter referred to as "the Constitution") require that there must be a dispute between the Federation and the States before this Court can exercise its original jurisdiction. They argued further that the dispute must involve any question of law or fact on which the existence or extent of a legal right depends. That there is no dispute apparent from the Statement of Claim to justify this action. The Court, therefore, lacks the jurisdiction to hear the case.

The plaintiff contends that in determining whether this Court has the jurisdiction to hear the case it needs to look at the Statement of Claim and the relief sought by it only, as laid down by the decision of this Court in Adeyemi v Opeyori, (1976) 10 N.S.C. 455 at p. 464 per Idigbe, JSC and Izenkwe v Nnadozie, 14 WACA 361. He stated that the dispute or controversy which brought about the action relates to the discharge by the President of the Federal Republic of Nigeria of his responsibilities under section 162 subsection (2) of the Constitution, that the action is necessary mainly because there is a very serious dispute between the Federal Government and some of the State governments as to the seaward boundary of the States which are by the sea. This in turn creates a controversy as to whether natural resources located offshore of the Nigerian coastal belt must be treated as Federal or belonging to the littoral States. It is submitted that paragraphs 8 and 10 of the Statement of Claim read together establish the dispute between the Federal government and the States which challenge the jurisdiction of the Court on the ground that there is no dispute.

Now section 232 subsection (1) of the Constitution provides:-

"232 (1) The Supreme Court shall, to the exclusion of any other Court, have original jurisdiction in any dispute between the Federation and a State or between States if and in so far

146

as that dispute involved any question (whether of law or fact) on which the existence or extent of a legal right depends".

It follows, therefore, that for this Court to exercise its original jurisdiction in a civil case between the Federation and State(s) or between States, there must be:-

(a)   a dispute between the Federation and a State or States;

(b)   the dispute must involve a question of law or fact or both; and

(c)   the dispute must pertain to the existence or extent of a legal right.

What constitutes a dispute under section 212 subsection (1) of the Constitution of the Federal Republic of Nigeria, 1979, which has exactly the same provisions as section 232 sub-section (1) in question had been considered by this Court in the cases of the Attorney-General of Bendel State v. Attorney-General of the Federation & 22 Ors. (1981) 10 S.C. I and A-G of the Federation v A-G of Imo State & 2 Ors, (1983), 4 N.C.L.R. 178. In Attorney-General of Bendel State's case, Bello, JSC (as he then was) stated as follows on pp. 48 to 49 thereof:-
"To invoke the original jurisdiction of this Court there must be a dispute as so qualified between the Federation and a State or between States.

The issue of jurisdiction was contested on three grounds. Firstly, that there is no dispute which affected the interest of the Federation and Bendel State between the plaintiff (Bendel State) and the Federation.

Secondly,...I think the first point may be easily disposed of from the definition of the word "dispute". The Oxford Universal Dictionary defined it as 'the act of arguing against, controversy, debate, contention as to rights, claims and the like or on a matter of opinion'.

I also held as follows on p. 320 thereof:-

"It is a well established principle of the interpretation of a constitution that the words of a constitution are not to be read with stultifying narrowness. United States v. Classic, 313 U.S 299 and Hafia Rabiu v. The State, (1980) 8-11 S.C. 130 a pp. 148-149. The word 'dispute' in section 212 (1) should therefore be given such meaning that will effectuate rather than defeat the purpose of that section of the Constitution.

Webster's New Twentieth Century Dictionary, 2nd Edition, provides that 'dispute' is synonymous with controversy, quarrel, argument, disagreement and contention.

147

It is clear that paragraph 10 of the Statement of Defence in this case, which is quoted above, has expressly averred that there is a dispute or controversy between the Plaintiff and the 3rd, 6th, 9th, 10th, 24th, 27th and 28th defendants on the facts averred in paragraph 8 of the Statement of Claim. By the decision of this court in the case of Adeyemi v. Operyori, (supra), those averments are to be taken as true ex-facie for the purpose of the present exercise. I am, therefore, satisfied that there is a dispute between the plaintiff and the littoral States as defen-dants in this case.

The next question is: whether the dispute involved a question of law or fact or both? The preliminary objectors have variously argued that the plaintiff's claim has not established the existence of a valid dispute whether of law or fact nor disclosed the existence or extent of a legal right.

The dispute, as stated in the Statement of Claim concerns the sharing of the "Federation Account" based on the principle of derivation as provided under section 162 (2) to determine who benefits or shares in the allocation of revenue accruing from the natural resources located offshore the coastal area of Nigeria. In my opinion, the dispute involves at least a question of Law, (if not fact), which is the interpretation of Section 162 subsection (2) of the constitution, in particular the provision there of which directly affects the littoral states and indirectly the non-littoral States.

The last question is: whether the dispute pertains to the existence or extent of a legal right? The short answer to this is provided by the dictum of Bello, JSC in the case of A-G Bendel State v A-G of the Federation & 22 Ors, (supra) at p. 50 thereof, viz.

"It is clear from the two sections of the 1979 Constitution that the plaintiff has a constitutional right to a portion of any amount standing to the credit of the Federation Account. It follows, therefore, that the dispute between the plaintiff (Bendel State) and the Federation involves a question on which the extent of a constitutional right of the plaintiff depends. I do not think any authority is required to say that a constitutional right is a legal right within the purview of section 212 of the (1979) Constitution" (interpolation mine for clarity).

The next point on jurisdiction is that this Court has no jurisdiction to entertain plaintiff's claim or gain the relief sought or to interpret section 162 (2) of the Constitution including the proviso thereof because the dispute is non-justiciable.

As has been shown above, section 231 (1) of the Constitution vests this Court with the jurisdiction to determine any dispute between the Federation and the States. In addition, section 6 (1) of the Constitution vests in the Supreme Court the judicial powers of the Federation and subsection (6) thereof provides that the power vested

148

"(a)   shall extend, notwithstanding anything to the contrary in this constitution to all inherent powers and sanctions of a court of law;

(b)   shall extend to all matters between persons, or between government or ... and to any person in Nigeria, and to actions and proceedings relating thereof, for the determination of any question as to the civil rights and obligations of that person.

These provisions clearly show that this Court has the jurisdiction to interpret not only the provisions of section 162 subsection (2) but also all the other provisions of the Constitution whether on appeal or in exercise of its original jurisdiction under section 232 subsection (1). The dispute in the present case, as shown above, involves at least the interpretation of section 162 sub-section (2) of the Constitution. Any issue which calls for the interpretation of the Constitution is obviously justiciable unless otherwise provided by the constitution. The end result of the interpretation may not entitle the plaintiff to the relief sought but then that is another matter, and it is not a ground to contend that the claim is not justiciable or that the Court lacks the jurisdiction to hear the case.

Misjoinder of Parties

It has been canvassed that the 28 non-littoral States joined by the plaintiff in the action are wrongly joined since they have no seaward boundary and ought to be struck out from the case. It is also argued that since the action is not properly constituted it is incurably defective on grounds of the misjoinder of the non-littoral states.

The plaintiff submits that all the States of the Federation are likely to be affected by whatever answer this Court gives to the true meaning of the proviso to section 162 (2) of the constitution. Reliance is placed on the judgement of this court in the case of A-G of Bendel State v Attorney-General of the Federation; (1981) ALL NLR (Part 2) 1 where it was held:

"Any party that might be affected by the decision of the Court in a suit ought to be joined. It is therefore proper to join the States that are satisfied with the manner and form the 1981 Act was enacted even though there is no apparent dispute between them and the plaintiff."

The same issue as canvassed here by the preliminary objectors was raised in A-G of Bendel State v A-G of the Federation & 22 Ors, (supra). Fatayi-Williams, CJN dealt with the question as follows on p. 24 thereof:-

149

Moreover, since all and each of the States in the Federation have a stake in what its legal share of the revenue should be it is only fair and just that such states should be joined in the suit.

Some of the States may agree that the procedure should be challenged while others may not. It is for each state to come to court and say so and for Court to adjudicate as to whether any legal right pertaining thereto has been infringed during the exercise of the legislative power by the National Assembly. For this reason I hold that there is a dispute between the government of Bendel State and the Federal Government, that the dispute involves not only questions of law, of fact, but also the constitutional right of the Bendel State Government. Furthermore, it is fair, just and proper for all the other defen-dants sued or joined by the order of court to be heard when the claims of Bendel State are being considered by this court. (Italics mine).

I need only to add that it is possible that the decision given by this Court, in the event of its coming to consider the substantive issue in this case, is likely to affect the non-littoral States. The proviso to section 162 subsection (2) of the constitution relates to the distribution of the Federation Account and the non-littoral States, are constitutionally entitled to share in the distribution of the Federation Account. I am satisfied, therefore, that there is no misjoinder of the parties in making the non-littoral states parties to this case since they are necessary parties to the case.

Seaward Boundary of Littoral State:

It has been contended that the plaintiff's claim seeking this Court to determine the boundary of the littoral States is not justiciable since the Supreme Court has no jurisdiction to determine the boundaries of the states and that only the National Boundaries Commission has the power to do so. It is also argued that the delimitation, demarcation or adjustment of the boundaries between States is the responsibility of the Executive or the Legislature, and since under the constitution there is separation of powers between the three arms of government, namely, the Executive, the Legislature and the Judiciary, the Supreme Court will be usurping the function of the Executive or the Legislature, if it should grant the relief sought by the plaintiff by determining the seaward boundaries of the littoral states. It is further canvassed that the determination of the coastal boundary of a state touches on the Law of the Sea and therefore comes under the realm of international law.

In reply, the plaintiff submitted that States are made up of areas stated against them in the Second Schedule to the Constitution as provided by section 3 subsection (2) of the Con-

150

stitution. That the area of each state are made up of local government areas but there are no laws for which the Supreme Court lacks jurisdiction. That only the International Court of Justice at the Hague has such jurisdiction to determine the seaward boundary of the states without boundaries; the littoral states have seaward boundaries and these are what the Court is being called upon to determine. It is submitted that this can be done by examining the provisions of the Constitution.

The main thrust of this suit is the interpretation of the constitution and not the determination of Inter-State boundaries as provided by the National Boundary Commission etc. Act cap. 238 of the laws of the Federation, 1990. Section 3 sub-section (1) of the Constitution provides that there shall be 36 States in Nigeria; and subsection (2) thereof provides:-
"(2) Each State of Nigeria named in the first column of part 1 of the First Schedule to this constitution shall consist of the area shown opposite thereto in the second column of that Schedule."
Surely, this Court is competent to interprete these provisions of the constitution. In doing so it is not usurping the powers of the Legislature or the Executive but exercising its interpretative power as given unto it by the Constitution.

In such a situation the court is not also exercising the power given to the National Boundary Commission under the National Boundary Commission etc. Act Cap. 238 but exercising its powers under the Constitution which could be same or concurrent with that of the commission. I see no conflict in this case between the powers of the Supreme Court and those of the commission. If there were any, the Constitution being supreme to the Act its provisions will in that case prevail over those of the Act - see Section 1 subsection (3) of the Constitution.

There cannot be a boundary dispute between the federation, which consists of all the states of the Federation, and individual States whether littoral or otherwise since the boundaries are the same - see Section 2 subsection (2) of the Constitution which provides that "Nigeria shall be a Federation consisting of States and a Federal Capital Territory.

The seaward boundary of Nigeria as well as the international boundaries of Nigeria are the subject of international law in the event of dispute between Nigeria and any of its neighbouring countries or between Nigeria and any other nation state vis a vis its territorial waters of the high seas. Nigerian Courts inclu-ding the Supreme Court may not have jurisdiction over such disputes but international tribunals like the International Court of Justice in the Hague do have such juridiction.

The situation in this case is not the same. Any dispute between the federation and the State or states is within the ambit of the jurisdiction of the Supreme Court as provided by section 232 subsection (1) of the constitution. It is, therefore, a misconception to argue that the dispute in this case is beyond the jurisdiction of the Supreme Court and can only be determined by an international tribunal.

Cause of Action

The 4th and 6th defendants contend that the action brought by the plaintiff does not disclose a reasonable cause of action. It is also argued that the action is premature as the President of the Federal Republic of Nigeria has not yet tabled any proposal for revenue allocation before the National Assembly in accordance with the provisions of section 162 subsection (2) of the Constitution. Also that there is no legislation, the interpretation of which will enable the Supreme Court to determine the seaward boundary of the littoral State.

A cause of action has been defined to mean the fact or facts which establishes or gives rise to a right of action and that it is a factual situation which gives a person the right to judicial relief - see Egbe v Adefarasin, (1987) 1 NWLR (Part 47)1. It is sufficient for a court to hold that a cause of action is reasonable once the statement of claim in a case discloses some cause of action or some questions fit to be decided by a judge notwithstanding that the case is weak or not likely to succeed. The fact that the course of action is weak or unlikely to succeed is not ground to strike it out - see Moore v Lawson, 31 TLR 418 CA; Wenlock v Moloney, (1965) W.L.R. 1238 and Irene Thomas & Ors v Olufoseye, (1986) 1 NWLR (Part 18) 669.

I, therefore hold that there is a reasonable cause of action in the present case because the statement of claim has disclosed enough facts to give rise to a cause of action.

Although the President of the Federal Republic of Nigeria is yet to present a bill to the National Assembly on revenue allocation in accordance with the provisions of section 162 (2) of the constitution there is already an "existing" law on the subject viz Allocation of Revenue (Federation Account, etc). Act, Cap. 16 of the Laws of Nigeria 1990 as amended by the Allocation of Revenue (Federation Account etc) (Amendment) Decree (Act) 1992 No. 106 of 1992. In my opinion, the action is not therefore proved by mere reference to the provisions of the constitution. On the other hand, if the action is premature the likely event is that plaintiff will fail to prove his case;

Locus Standi

The 9th defendant argues that the plaintiff lacks locus standi to bring the action because the Statement of Claim does not plead that the plaintiff's civil right and obligation, with regard to the plaintiffs share of the Federation Account, has been affected by the provision of the Allocation of Revenue (Federation Account etc) (Amendment) Decree No. 106 of 1992.

The 4th defendant contends that the plaintiff has no locus standi because he pleaded in paragraph 1 of the Statement of Claim that he brings the action as a representative of government of the Federal Republic of Nigeria which consists of the Executive, Legislature and Judiciary. For him to have locus standi he must show that each of the three arms of government has given him its consent to bring a representative action in accordance with Order 3 rule 1 and 5 rule (1) (a) of the Supreme Court rules, 1985.

In reply, the plaintiff submits that section 232 (1) of the Constitution vests this Court with special jurisdiction to deal with disputes between the Federation and State or States and between States. The case is between the Federation and the States and not as between individuals. That the defendants have overlooked this fact. Citing A-G of Ondo State v A-G of the Federation & Ors, 1983 NSCC 612, the plaintiff submitted that once it is shown that there is a real dispute between the parties in the case then, a locus standi has been established.

I have already held in this ruling that there is a justiciable dispute in this case involving the legal right of the plaintiff. The Federal Government has the constitutional right and legal obligation to have a share in the Federation Account. It needs only to indicate that a justiciable dispute exists between it and the defendants to have the locus to sue A-G of Bendel State v A-G of the Federation & 22 Ors. (Supra) at p. 157 per Obaseki, JSC.

To argue that the plaintiff must show that he has the consent of the Federal Legislature and the Federal Judiciary to bring this action is to ignore the provisions of section 20 of the Supreme Court Act, 424, which states-

20.   Any proceedings before the Supreme Court arising out of the dispute referred to in section 212 (1) (i.e. section 232 (1) of the Constitution and brought by or against the Federation or a State shall:

(a)   in the case of the Federation be brought in the name of the Attorney-General of the Federation,

153

(b)   in the case of a State be brought in the name of the
Attorney-General of the State.

Political Question

The 9th defendant argues that the case raises political
question because of the averments in the Statement of Claim
by the plaintiff and the Statement of Defence by the defendants. Constitutional Law Cases and Materials, 7th Edition, by Professor Dowling and Gunther was cited with particular reference to p. 163 thereof. The defendant also referred to "Toward Neutral Principles of Constitutional Law",
by Professor Wechster, an article published in 73 Harvard
Law Review, 1,7,9, Selected Essays 1938 - 62 (1963) at pp.
463 and 468.

The 4th defendant submits that section 162 subsection
(3) of the Constitution gives the National Assembly the
power to prescribe a new revenue allocation formula and
the plaintiff is asking the Supreme Court to do the same by
urging the Court to provide the manner of distribution of
the Federation Account, thus usurping the powers of the
National Assembly. That the matters which the National
Assembly would take into consideration in prescribing a
new formula for the allocation of the Federation Account
are political. That the Supreme Court cannot deal with a
political question. The case of Onuoha v Okafor & Ors,
(1983) 14 NSCC is cited in support of the argument.

The plaintiff replies that it is untenable to canvass that
the Statement of Claim raises a political issue. He argues
that the plaintiff's claim is a justiciable dispute which satis-
fies the criteria laid down by this Court in the case of A-G of
Ondo State v A-G of the Federation & Ors., (supra) per
Nnamani, JSC.

The question may be asked: does the dispute as to the
interpretation of the provisions of section 162 subsection
(2) of the Constitution not involve any question (whether
of law or fact) on which the existence or extent of a legal
right depend? The answer to the question has been given in
the affirmative earlier in this ruling. There is undoubtedly a
dispute as stated in paragraphs 8 & 10 of the Statement of
Claim and substantially admitting of specific relief - see
A-G of Bendel State's case (supra)

Procedural Irregularity

The 27th defendant raised the preliminary objection that it is not for the plaintiff to start the action by filling a Statement of Claim instead of issuing an originating summons. He refers to Order 3 rules 2 (2) and 6 (1) of the Supreme Court Rules, 1985 in support of the objection.

The plaintiff replies that Order 3 rules 6 (1) of the Supreme Court Rules, 1985 is permissive and not mandatory. That there is, therefore, no justification for the defendant to say that the case must be commenced by originating summons.

Now, Order 3 rule 6 (1) states:-

"In any proceedings where the Court has original jurisdiction, any party claiming any legal or equitable right and the determination of the question whether it is entitled to the right depends on the construction of the Constitution or any other enactment may apply for the issue of an originating summons for the determination of such question of construction and for a declaration as to the right claimed and for any further or other relief".

The objection raises only a procedural irregularity...

www.ingramcontent.com/pod-product-compliance
Lightning Source LLC
Chambersburg PA
CBHW021829020426
42334CB00014B/554